GLOBAL ORGANIZATIONS

The United Nations

GLOBAL ORGANIZATIONS

The African Union

The Arab League

The Association of Southeast Asian Nations

The Caribbean Community and Common Market

The European Union

The International Atomic Energy Agency

The Organization of American States

The Organization of Petroleum
Exporting Countries

The United Nations

The United Nations Children's Fund

The World Bank and
the International Monetary Fund

The World Health Organization

The World Trade Organization

GLOBAL ORGANIZATIONS

The United Nations

Kirsten Nakjavani Bookmiller

Series Editor
Peggy Kahn
University of Michigan–Flint

CHELSEA HOUSE
PUBLISHERS
An imprint of Infobase Publishing

For My Sweet Sebastian:
The World Awaits

The United Nations
Copyright © 2008 by Infobase Publishing

Chelsea House
An imprint of Infobase Publishing
132 West 31st Street
New York NY 10001

Library of Congress Cataloging-in-Publication Data
Bookmiller, Kirsten Nakjavani.
  The United Nations / Kirsten Bookmiller.
    p. cm. — (Global organizations)
  ISBN: 978-0-7910-9540-9 (hardcover)
  1. United Nations. I. Title. II. Series.

JZ4984.5.B67 2008
341.23—dc22   2007042710

Series design by Erik Lindstrom
Cover design by Ben Peterson

Printed in the United States of America

Bang KT 10 9 8 7 6 5 4 3 2 1

This book is printed on acid-free paper.

All links and Web addresses were checked and verified to be correct at the time of publication. Because of the dynamic nature of the Web, some addresses and links may have changed since publication and may no longer be valid.

CONTENTS

INTRODUCTION

The Story of the Tied-up Gun

NEW YORK CITY IS FAMOUS FOR HUNDREDS OF LANDMARKS that dot its many neighborhoods and well-known skyline. The ice rink at Rockefeller Center, the bright neon lights of Times Square, and the Empire State Building are just a few New York City destinations that attract millions of tourists each year.

There is one particular sculpture, however, that also draws visitors from around the world. It is neither the biggest structure in the city nor the brightest nor the most beautiful. Yet anyone who sees this memorable piece of public art immediately wants to have a photograph of it.

It is a large black handgun. But this is not a sculpture of just any gun. This firearm has its barrel tied in a knot at the end, rendering the weapon useless. The barrel is not aimed straight ahead but points upward toward the sky.

The knotted gun was a gift given to the United Nations by Luxembourg and can be found at the entrance of the organization's headquarters. Made by sculptor Fredrik Reuterswärd in memory of singer John Lennon, about 20 identical statues, including this one, are placed around the world to promote non-violence.

This giant revolver, titled *Non-Violence*, was given as a gift to the United Nations (UN) by member country Luxembourg in 1988. The artwork's eye-level pedestal stands on the path to the UN headquarters' visitor entrance, just beyond the ring of 192 member-country flags and the tall black UN gates. Sculptor Fredrik Reuterswärd created the piece upon learning of the gun murder of his friend and former Beatles member John Lennon.

Each year more than 700,000 visitors pass by this sculpture, and every few minutes, the world's citizens pause to have their picture taken in front of this twisted gun before or after taking a UN tour. It might be a group of French children, who will shyly ask if a few Israeli teenagers will snap their photo while standing before the turned-up weapon. Next, the same young Israelis politely interrupt a Chilean family walking by and inquire if someone will do the same for them, hopefully also capturing the UN buildings in the background. And so it goes, nationality after nationality, getting a snapshot on their digital cameras and cell phones of the gun with its barrel tied in a knot at the end.

What is it about this gun that grabs everyone's interest and imagination? Is it the world of possibility that the sculpture represents? Will one day all the guns of the world be tied up? Can the human family bring to a close its long history of extraordinary pain and suffering as a result of senseless violence? Or does it represent a sweet fantasy, nice to ponder, but never a real possibility?

All the perils and all the promises of achieving global peace exist in the buildings that sit just behind this work of art. And while young and old from around the world swap cameras to get a souvenir of their visit to the United Nations, they rest their hopes upon the UN's 192 countries to get as close as possible to a life where guns are knotted forever.

Introduction
to the UN

MORE THAN 50 MILLION MEN, WOMEN, AND CHILDREN LAY dead on battlefields and in thousands of communities. Forty countries had fought on six continents and on all of the world's oceans. Millions of people were homeless and without food, clothing, or jobs. A seemingly interminable war had raged for six years, with the conflict slowly grinding to a halt in Europe, but no end in sight in East Asia.

This was the world as diplomats from 51 countries knew it when they met in San Francisco, California, in April 1945 to create the UN. They came together to form a new organization to provide peace and security for all countries, large and small. Sadly, many of these representatives had not only experienced World War II but also the horrors of the first war fought just 25 years previously. This earlier Great War—as it was known then—claimed at least 15 million lives directly and 20 million more indirectly. So it was not surprising that the San Francisco participants began the United Nations Charter with the following pledge: "WE THE PEOPLES OF THE UNITED NATIONS determined to save succeeding generations from the scourge of war, which twice in our lifetime has brought untold sorrow to mankind . . . "

Today the UN has grown to 192 member states, encompassing every country on the globe. While the framers of the UN Charter could not have envisioned many of the challenges of the early twenty-first century, this unique international institution is more relevant today than ever.

Being safe in our time is no longer just about preventing war. A case in point is Earth's steadily rising average temperatures, known as global warming. It is increasingly believed to cause extreme weather, such as catastrophic droughts, heat waves, and hurricanes like the one that destroyed New Orleans and other surrounding areas in 2005. Infectious diseases, carried across borders by the 3.3 billion people who fly internationally every year, pose another threat. In just a few weeks in 2003, severe acute respiratory syndrome (SARS) spread globally from its initial outbreak in Southeast Asia, carried by individuals on intercontinental flights traveling for business, family visits and weddings, or returning home to their respective countries. The HIV/AIDS pandemic, devastating whole communities, is far more deadly than any war. Food shortages, lack of clean drinking water, and poor medical care still cost millions of lives. And while war is no longer commonly waged between countries, civil warfare still results in staggering losses of life and human rights atrocities.

While those gathered in San Francisco more than 60 years ago could not have predicted all of today's vexing transnational problems, they still succeeded in creating a world body that fits many of the needs of our own times. According to Article 1 of the UN Charter, the organization's purposes are:

1. to maintain international peace and security;
2. to develop friendly relations among nations;
3. to achieve international co-operation in solving international problems of an economic, social, cultural, or humanitarian character, and promoting respect for human rights and for fundamental freedoms for all; and
4. to be a center for harmonizing the actions of nations in attainment of these common ends.

The last goal is the key to understanding the singular importance of the UN. The UN's role as an international center to discuss any common concern, whatever its nature, makes it unique among the more than 300 intergovernmental organizations that exist in the world today. Intergovernmental organizations (IGOs) are permanent associations of countries (rather than temporary conferences). They have founding documents similar to a constitution, formal bodies like the executive and legislative branches of the U.S. government, and an administrative bureaucracy to help implement decisions. The governments of these countries, also known as states (not to be confused with the 50 states of the United States), form these organizations because they believe that there are shared challenges that can only be addressed by having many governments meeting full-time, in constant session, year after year.

IGOs can be classified by their membership as well as their function. The Organization of Petroleum Exporting Countries (OPEC), for instance, is restricted to those countries that export oil and focuses solely on issues related to oil prices and supply. The European Union (EU), on the other hand, consists only of European countries with democratic political systems and open economies but is multipurpose in scope. It helps its member states cooperate on a wide variety of issues, ranging from a common currency to shared defense.

Some organizations, like the World Health Organization or the World Trade Organization, are in principle open to any state of the international community, but concentrate just on health and trade issues, respectively.

The UN is different. It is the only intergovernmental organization in the world today that is both international in membership *and* dedicated to responding through one organization to all of the global community's challenges. The UN is the world hub of cooperation, humankind's political and diplomatic heart. Representatives from large countries, like the People's Republic of China and India, with more than 1 billion inhabitants each, meet with envoys from small states such as the tiny Pacific state of Nauru, with only 13,000 citizens. Poor and wealthy states' delegates confer in hallways and conference rooms. Governments with no armies sit at the same table with military powerhouses. Illiteracy, starvation, infectious disease, pollution, the buying and selling of human beings, infant mortality, child soldiers, poverty, overpopulation, unequal economic development, the drug trade, refugees and internally displaced persons, dangerous working conditions, disappearing cultures, the digital divide, human rights violations, terrorism, war, and nuclear proliferation are but a few of the issues on the agenda every day at the UN.

The UN has helped humankind in countless ways, although many of its successes don't make the nightly TV news. The UN system has completely wiped out smallpox and eliminated polio around the globe except in six countries. It has helped bring safe drinking water to more than 2 billion people, and it has aided 50 million refugees. More than 170 peace agreements have been negotiated under the world body's auspices. Coupled with its more than 60 peacekeeping missions and other peace initiatives, the UN has been a major player in reducing the number of armed conflicts and genocides. The organization has built a cooperative network among the

Medical assistance has become one of the most recognizable missions of the UN. The organization has helped eradicate smallpox and limited the spread of polio, while also administering vaccines to thousands of people in need. Here, Pakistani and Chinese forces help bolster medical outreach in rural areas of the African country Liberia.

states of the world by facilitating more than 500 international agreements on issues as wide-ranging as tobacco advertising to fishing. It played a major role in making colonization, or the subjugation of peoples by an outside power, unacceptable behavior in international relations. More than 80 independent states emerged as a result. The UN has additionally advanced democracy in nearly 100 countries by providing electoral support during periods of historic political change, such as the end of the racist apartheid regime in South Africa; after the withdrawal of colonial power Indonesia from East Timor;

and following the fall of the extremist Taliban government in Afghanistan. And, thanks to the UN's promotion of human rights, the world's attention is focused on the injustices faced by citizens everywhere.

Yet for all of the UN's many accomplishments, even its most passionate supporters admit that it can do better. Place names such as Darfur, Rwanda, and Bosnia are as well known for the UN's political paralysis as for the terrible genocides that occurred in these war zones. Moreover, the United States and its allies launched the war in Iraq in the spring of 2003 against the wishes of the majority of the UN. Critics charge that the organization's decision-making structure, especially the Security Council, is completely outdated, more reflective of the mid-twentieth-century power landscape than today's political realities. Great powers, particularly the United States, selfishly dominate the organization, or the smaller and poorer ones are running the place, depending on the point of view. The institution itself is burdened by financial debt, and many regard the bureaucracy as inefficient and unwieldy. Some international civil servants who work within the UN Secretariat have faced corruption charges related to the Iraq Oil for Food program, designed to alleviate the suffering of everyday Iraqis caused by UN-imposed economic sanctions before the fall of Saddam Hussein's government in 2003.

Despite these challenges, for many the UN is still the place where the global citizenry's hopes for a peaceful and healthier future can be realized. Perhaps this is best expressed by the South Korean diplomat Ban Ki-moon, who became the UN secretary-general in 2007:

For the Korean people, the UN flag was and remains a beacon of better days to come. There are countless stories of that faith. One belongs to me. In 1956, when the Cold War was raging around the world, as a young boy of 12, I was chosen to read out a public message, on behalf of my elementary school, addressed to the Secretary-General of the United Nations, Mr. Dag Hammarskjöld. We urged him to help the people of a certain faraway European country in their fight for freedom and democracy. I hardly understood the deeper meaning of the message. But I knew that the UN was there for help in times of need. . . . I earnestly hope that young boys and girls of today will grow up knowing that the UN is working hard to build a better future for them.[1]

Starting Somewhere: The League of Nations

. . . [T]his is only one hospital, one single station; there are hundreds of thousands in Germany, hundreds of thousands in France, hundreds of thousands in Russia. How senseless is everything that can ever be written, done, or thought, when such things are possible. It must be all lies and of no account when the culture of a thousand years could not prevent this stream of blood being poured out. . . .[2]

—The character Paul Bäumer from
All Quiet on the Western Front

FOR HUNDREDS OF YEARS, COUNTRIES WAGED WAR AGAINST one another. And every time, despite the countless lives lost, governments assumed a business-as-usual approach once the peace treaty was signed. But something changed after World

War I. World leaders made a historic decision. They decided that the great challenges of peace and war could no longer be left to individual countries to fix on their own. They needed a permanent organization to make lasting peace possible. As a result, the League of Nations, the UN's direct forerunner, was born.

The League of Nations, which officially existed from 1920 to 1946, was the world's first-ever attempt at an international organization dedicated to ensuring the security of its member countries and promoting peace among them. While many Americans think of the league as a failure and perhaps even a historical dinosaur—with little to no importance to understanding our own times—the truth is quite the opposite. The League of Nations established many of the game rules by which the UN operates today, as well as provided valuable lessons in its failures. Still, after so many centuries of bloodshed, what was it about World War I that finally pushed countries to try another way to an enduring peace?

THE WAR TO END ALL WARS

World War I lasted for more than four terrible years, formally beginning on August 5, 1914, and ending with a cease-fire on November 11, 1918. The Great War, as it was known at the time, was utterly devastating in so many different ways that it was frequently referred to as "the war to end all wars." Sadly, this optimism turned out to be misplaced, but one can understand why people wanted to believe it at the time. Never before in human history had a single conflict involved such a magnitude of peoples and countries from all over the globe simultaneously, ultimately bringing in every continent save Antarctica.

Initially, the players included the traditional European powers, with Great Britain, France, and Russia (later to be referred to as "the Allies") on one side, and Germany and Austria-Hungary (named the "Central Powers") on the other. In just the first two weeks of the conflict, 10 percent of Europe's population was mobilized, equaling 20 million men. Devastating Europe-wide conflicts were nothing new, unfortunately. Within a few short months, however, and for the first time ever in world history, the bloodshed broke out of its regional confines and spiraled into a globe-spanning war. By the time the war concluded four years later, 26 countries from the Americas (including the United States after 1917), Asia, and Europe had joined the Allied side while Austria-Hungary, Bulgaria, Germany, and the Ottoman Empire formed the core of the Central Powers.

World War I's global geographic and human sweep was not the only unique aspect of the conflict. Combat technology had also been dramatically transformed. By 1914, the second industrial revolution was in full swing, ensuring that this war would not be a traditional one employing horses and bayonets. All of today's instruments of modern warfare, including the military use of airplanes and submarines and tanks; machine guns; grenades; and biological and chemical weapons, including mustard gas and deadly chlorine, became routinely used for the first time during the Great War.

The combination of unmatched numbers of soldiers fighting on a global battlefield with the mechanized warfare of the industrial age resulted in the deadliest and most destructive conflict humanity had ever experienced to that point. At the Battle of Verdun alone, Germany and France both lost more than 300,000 men. The total numbers killed and injured in the Great War will never be known, and estimates vary widely. Figures for soldiers killed range between 7 and 8.5 million and the injured counted at over 20 million. Nearly 2 million were never found. Total civilian (noncombatant) casualties are also calculated to be in the millions. Many of those who survived the conflict were permanently blinded by deadly gases, lost arms and legs, and were forever psychologically traumatized by their experiences. These shocking statistics do not include the deadly Spanish flu outbreak that swept the globe between 1918 and 1920, an epidemic claiming the lives of 50 million more people.

After the assassination of Archduke Ferdinand, heir to the Austrian-Hungarian Empire, various countries were obliged to take sides in the first global war in history. Because advances in technology had modernized weapons to make them more destructive, homes and buildings were turned to rubble in battles and much of Europe, like this French church used as a field hospital during the war, was in ruins.

The heartbreak felt by many Americans after the loss of 3,000 individuals in the World Trade Center and Pentagon terrorist attacks of September 11, 2001, puts into perspective the trauma people living during World War I must have felt. It also makes sense that there was a very strong desire within the world's corridors of power to take concerted action so that such a human-caused catastrophe would never happen again. Thus the League of Nations was born.

THE BIRTH OF THE LEAGUE OF NATIONS

U.S. President Woodrow Wilson (president from 1913 to 1921) is often popularly credited with being the "father" of the league and, in fact, was awarded the Nobel Peace Prize for his efforts. Though Wilson's contributions were many and significant, statesmen from around the world were consumed by the same concern: How can world peace be achieved? How can all members of the global community feel safe, irrespective of how large or small they are, or their power status? For these politicians and diplomats, the answer could only be one thing: the unprecedented creation of a permanent world body that all countries would belong to, in which they would collectively band together to make all members feel secure. The thinking was that one country's aggression against another would be countered with overwhelming diplomatic, economic, and military resistance by the rest of the organization's members, in what is known as collective security.

In the 1800s, formal organizations between countries had sprung up for the first time to promote regional and global economic, social, and technical cooperation. However, no government had proposed such a plan for addressing the challenges of peace and war. Countries feared handing over their final authority, or sovereignty, of their national militaries to some larger world body. While thinkers for centuries had pondered the idea of collective security, it took the tremendous bloodletting of World War I to be the final catalyst for real action.

As millions fought on the battlefronts in Europe, the Middle East, and Africa, President Wilson delivered his famous "Fourteen Points" speech to the U.S. Congress on January 8, 1918. He urged that "[a] general association of nations must be formed under specific covenants for the purpose of affording

The last of President Woodrow Wilson's "fourteen points" in his speech of the same name, presented the idea of an international organization where countries would work together to prevent conflicts similar to the ones that led to World War I. This organization, called the League of Nations, was integrated into the peace agreement ending the war, but the U.S. Senate voted against this agreement, choosing not to take part in the League. Pictured from left to right: David Lloyd George, of Great Britain; Vittorio Orlando, of Italy; Georges Clemenceau, of France; and Woodrow Wilson, of the United States.

mutual guarantees of political independence and territorial integrity to great and small powers alike." In the following months, President Wilson actively pushed for the league's establishment, insisting that it should be the first agenda item at the Paris Peace Conference and part of the resulting peace treaty. By the time Wilson arrived in Paris for the opening of the conference in January 1919, he was greeted by millions of Europeans as a hero. Six months later, in June 1919, the

Treaty of Versailles (named for the French royal palace where the conference was held) finally and officially ended the Great War. It contained among its provisions the League of Nations Covenant, similar to a constitution, for this new world body.

In one of the most famous and astonishing treaty rejections in all of American history, the U.S. Senate voted down the Treaty of Versailles in November 1919 and again in March 1920. The Senate's rebuffs reflected the long-standing American fear of losing sovereignty, or control, over U.S. affairs, to a higher legal and political entity. As a result, the United States never joined Woodrow Wilson's League of Nations.

HOW THE LEAGUE WAS MEANT TO WORK

The statesmen at the Paris Peace Conference were starting from scratch. With nothing to work from but their own ideas and visions for how such a novel organization should be built, they struggled with many issues. The founders were also racing against the clock. Because the final document would include both the League of Nations constitution and the peace treaty to end the war, time was running out.

The resulting League of Nations Covenant is therefore a brief document of just 26 articles, compared to the later UN Charter's 111 articles. The covenant accepted the reality of a community of independent countries, and it did not press for a new, "one world" government where individual national governments would disappear. What was groundbreaking, however, was its pioneering call for the way the world's countries should inter-act with one another. In the covenant's preamble, the very first line urges its members "to not resort to war!" The document also calls for states to have "open, just and honorable" relations with one another, be guided by international law, and to respect any written agreements that they have with one another. For centuries, powerful countries did what they wanted when they wanted, including wielding violence, and the weaker countries had to accept whatever came their way. Until World War I came

The League of Nations became a great hope for people around the world as they recovered from the Great War. After the Treaty of Versailles was signed, the League held its first opening session in Switzerland. The meeting, however, was far from ideal as the United States refused to sign and take part in the League of Nations, while Germany and the USSR were not allowed to join until 1926 and 1934, respectively.

to pass, no international organization or law existed making such behavior illegal. Thus the principles enshrined in the League of Nations were a remarkable departure from how the world had previously approached questions of war and peace.

The league was headquartered in Geneva, Switzerland, and began operations in 1920. It started with 45 members from around the world and reached a high of 63. The covenant outlined a basic structure of an assembly, a secretariat, and a council. The League Assembly was the forum in which all members were represented (known as a plenary body), and each member had one vote, regardless of their country's size or power status. As it included the majority of states that existed at that time, the assembly was viewed as an important barometer of international public opinion.

The secretariat was the organization's administrative backbone, comprising 500 permanent employees from many different nationalities dedicated to the league's day-to-day operations. The secretariat housed diplomats, translators, international lawyers, disease experts, military specialists, economists, and the like, all working on behalf of the league rather than their home governments. At its top was the league's chief administrative officer, the secretary-general. The first was Sir Eric Drummond from Great Britain, serving from 1920 to 1933.

The council was at the heart of the organization's efforts to maintain international peace and security, with extensive powers assigned to it in determining how the league would respond in times of crisis. Like today's UN Security Council, there were permanent and temporary members, ensuring that the council did not become the playground of the large military powers, with no balancing of perspectives from smaller countries. During the league's existence, the number of permanent members changed, reflecting larger political developments. The original permanent four were Great Britain, France, Italy, and Japan, joined later by Germany and the Union of Soviet Socialist Republics (Soviet Union, or USSR).

All decisions in the assembly and the council had to be unanimous. This decision-making model meant that even if just one lone country wanted a particular measure under consideration to fail, it could simply vote no. Given that the league was charged with making important decisions about peace and war, the members were still sensitive about giving up their sovereignty over what had always been national concerns. There was one notable exception to the unanimity rule, however. When the council or the assembly was responding to an incident involving particular members, then those implicated members could not block the vote. They were parties with a vested interest in the outcome of a decision and the thinking was that they should not have a say.

In addition to the league assembly, secretariat, and council, the covenant called for the creation of a new international court, called the Permanent Court of International Justice (PCIJ). The PCIJ was history's first ongoing court dedicated to settling legal disputes and providing advisory opinions for governments in conflict. In recognizing the league's "Social Responsibilities" as one section was called, the covenant also established itself at the center of a web of technical, social, and humanitarian international bureaus, commissions, and national Red Cross societies. Many of these institutions would become the core of the UN specialized agencies, including the World Health Organization. The league's founding treaty identified specific areas of concern, including labor rights, trafficking of women and children, the drug trade, infectious disease, postwar reconstruction, communication, transportation, and commerce. It should be noted that the covenant was silent on the concept of human rights.

The covenant's greatest attention was given to maintaining peace between its members, in 10 of 26 articles. Believing that rushes to judgment, miscommunication, the very existence of military arms, and a void of impartial third parties all led to the outbreak of the Great War, the league's overall strategy was to prevent an "accidental war." When disputes erupted, members should resolve their differences peacefully. To provide a space so that contesting governments could calm down, the covenant also dictated that the parties could not legally resort to war (notice that war was not outlawed) for several months until the league took action. It was the organization's fervent hope that calmer heads would prevail during this cooling-off period.

If a party did not carry out the league's recommendations in good faith, then the covenant dictated that the offending country shall be "deemed to have committed an act of war against all other Members of the League." The council could authorize a collective response, including joint diplomatic, economic, communications, and military sanctions, or punishments, against the guilty party. Council authorization (or the assembly if the dispute was transferred) for group action would have to be unanimous, with the exception of the involved members, according to the covenant's voting rules.

THE LEAGUE IN REALITY

The 1920s were a golden period for the league. With the pain and sorrow of World War I still fresh on people's minds and the benefits of general economic prosperity, many were hopeful about the new organization's prospects. Almost from the outset, the league became a global leader in the economic, social, and humanitarian fields. By 1939, more than 60 percent of the league's budget was dedicated to humanitarian causes. The growth of international law between countries was also strengthened, as the league fostered the development of 120 new treaties and the world court heard 66 cases between states.

Yet these significant accomplishments cannot disguise the fact that the league was unable to halt the slide to an even more catastrophic and devastating conflict, World War II. By the 1930s, the world body witnessed its weakening position as the hub of international affairs. During this decade, a worldwide economic depression, starting with the 1929 stock-market crash in the United States, forced member states to look inward and focus on their own national interests, rather than seek cooperation with other countries.

Great powers, including several permanent members of the council, began to abandon the league or were expelled. In the 1930s, Germany, Italy, Japan, and the USSR, bent on military competition and territorial expansion, invaded other league members in blatant disregard of the league's founding principles. As none of these permanent council members could block league action against them according to covenant rules, they either withdrew or were kicked out. With the exception of France and the United Kingdom, who made secret deals with Italy and others as a way to protect their own national interests, all the major League Council members were now effectively sitting outside of the organization along with the United States.

The league, in the end merely a reflection of larger global political strains, would never have been able to stand up independently to these threats. By the time of Germany's increasing aggression, first against Czechoslovakia starting in the summer of 1938 and a full invasion of Poland in September 1939, the world was again on a direct collision course for a new European, and within a short time, global conflict.

Growing Pains:
The UN's Birth
and Evolution

This charter, like our own Constitution, will be expanded and improved as time goes on. No one claims that it is now a final or perfect instrument. It has not been poured into a fixed mold. Changing world conditions will require readjustments—but they will be the readjustments of peace and not of war.[3]

**—U.S. President Harry Truman at the closing of the
United Conference at San Francisco, June 1945**

BY THE LATE 1930S, THE LEAGUE OF NATIONS HAD UNDENI-ably collapsed. And for those people who had survived the 1914–1918 war just 20 years earlier, the unimaginable was happening again. The international community was spiraling

Despite the early successes of the League of Nations, it proved to be unsuccessful at preventing the unimaginable—WWII. The desperate global economic situation distracted leaders from league violations committed by Italy, Germany, Japan, and the USSR, leading to a global war that would be even more destructive than the first.

into another history-shattering conflict, even more deadly and catastrophic than the first. Between 1939 and 1942, a startling chain of events shook the world. Nazi Germany swept through much of Western and Eastern Europe. It occupied parts of France and relentlessly bombarded Britain. Germany's supporter, Italy, soon joined and the war spread into the Mediterranean, southeastern Europe, and the Middle East. By 1941, the Axis had a firm military grip on Europe in every direction of the compass, from west to east and north to south, and into North Africa as well. At the same time, Japan blazed a military path throughout Southeast Asia, first challenging Britain and France in their colonial holdings, and later the United States.

As the United States and its military allies, including Britain, China, France, and the Soviet Union, organized their military counteroffensives, something extraordinary happened. These powers also decided to make yet another attempt at a global security organization. Surprisingly, the league's failure did not sour the international community, and especially the great powers, from trying *again*.

THE UNITED NATIONS BECOMES A REALITY

It was yet another American president who began to champion the cause, President Franklin D. Roosevelt. Roosevelt had been fascinated with the idea of an international security organization ever since accompanying President Woodrow Wilson on his ocean voyage to Europe for the Treaty of Versailles negotiations as Wilson's assistant secretary of the navy. Even before the United States officially joined World War II following the December 1941 Pearl Harbor bombing, President Roosevelt set to work on putting his international political vision into motion. Laying the groundwork for the UN early on in the conflict significantly departed from the league's creation process. While President Wilson waited until the end of World War I to negotiate the league and built it directly into the peace treaties, Wilson's World War II counterpart started in the early months of the war itself, when no one even knew who would actually win it. Designing the United Nations therefore took several years, instead of six months, and the resulting plan was more deliberate, considered, and professional. UN discussions were also conducted in the open, while league talks were held in secret.

The cornerstone of Roosevelt's strategy was to build the new postwar version of the League of Nations in collaboration with the United States' three key wartime Allies: Britain, the Republic of China (before its 1949 Communist revolution), and the Soviet Union. In a 1943 radio address, the president explained his reasoning: "Britain, Russia, China and the United States and their allies represent more than three-quarters of the total population of the Earth. As long as these four [n]ations with great military power stick together in determination to keep the peace, there will be no possibility of an aggressor [n]ation arising to start another world war."[4]

The new body's outline emerged out of tough diplomatic bargaining as the four countries met in various combinations at several different conferences from October 1943 until February 1945. The name "United Nations," while originally referring to the Allied coalition, was proposed as the developing entity's name. The UN would retain the league's twin goals of maintaining international security while promoting cooperation among its sovereign members. Many of the decision-making bodies were also directly borrowed from the league, including a general assembly, a security council, a secretariat, and a court. Two new bodies were added. The pioneering Economic and Social Council, viewed as a counterpart to the Security Council, reflected the growing awareness of economic and social injustice as a major root of violence. The Trusteeship Council would assume responsibility for promoting self-rule for the vast majority of the world's population that still lived under colonialism.

The powers agreed to jettison the league's cumbersome unanimity rule but kept the League Council's permanent-temporary formula. The permanent five would include the four Allied powers of Britain, China, the Soviet Union, and the United States, plus a fifth seat for France, believing that the latter, although occupied by Germany, would ultimately join the table after the war. While the Soviets initially demanded that the Security Council's permanent members have a full and unlimited right to veto any matter that came before the council (having been expelled by the league for its 1939

(continues on page 34)

WHEN YOUR FAMILY EXPANDS FROM 51 TO 192, WHAT DO YOU DO WITH YOUR HOUSE?

When Oscar Schacter, who served with the UN Secretariat from its beginning in 1946, was asked what one of his more memorable professional mistakes had been, he told the following story. As the architects were drawing up sketches for the UN headquarters in New York City, they asked the new UN legal adviser how many total member countries they should plan for in the General Assembly building. Schacter recalls his response with a laugh: "An international lawyer would be expected to know how many sovereign states existed and were potential members. I confidently answered the architects (after checking some textbooks) that they could safely add twenty seats to the fifty-one." *

Accordingly, the UN facilities were designed and built to accommodate an organization with a maximum of 70 countries and 700 meetings per year. Today the site is bursting at the seams with 192 members and 8,000 meetings held annually! None of the founders could have predicted the breathtaking pace of decolonization in the first 20 years of the world body, and that 40 years later one of its major powers would itself collapse into 15 new states alone. The UN headquarters sits hemmed in on an 18-acre plot running along the East River between 42nd and 48th Streets in Manhattan.

How did the world home of the UN end up in New York City? Following the U.S. Congress's unanimous endorsement to have the United States serve as the national host of the new organization in December 1945 (quite a turnaround after the 1920 rejection of the League of Nations), the General Assembly accepted the American invitation at its first session held in London in February 1946.

New York City had not been among the top list of candidates when UN planners were scouting potential sites. Oil magnate John D. Rockefeller made an offer, however, that the organization couldn't refuse. He donated the East River parcel (later added onto by New York City) that was certainly not the high-priced and glamorous real estate that it is known for today. As the UN Web site itself describes the neighborhood: "The site chosen by the United Nations was a run-down area of slaughterhouses, light industry, and a railroad barge landing."

The main facilities were completed by 1952, and the site now includes four major buildings, including the 39-story Secretariat tower, the low and curving General Assembly building, the Conference building, and the Dag Hammarskjöld Library. The 50-year-old buildings show significant wear and tear and no longer meet fire and safety codes. In 2000, the UN approved an ambitious

(continues)

(continued)

renovation and expansion plan. The overhaul was originally sched-
uled to begin in 2008, but with intense squabbling over costs and
funding sources and the challenge of relocating during the renova-
tions, the refurbishing plan remains in doubt.

According to the headquarters agreement with the United
States, the site is considered international territory and the UN
has its own security, firefighting unit, and post office that issues UN
stamps. The site in New York is truly the center of world affairs.
Each year, 5,000 diplomats and world leaders arrive to partici-
pate in the annual sessions of the General Assembly; nearly 9,000
Secretariat staff members work there; more than 700,000 visitors
tour the headquarters; thousands of journalists are accredited
to cover the proceedings; and many more thousands of private
citizens from around the globe come to lobby national representatives. For your own virtual tour of the United Nations, visit *http://
www.un.org/Pubs/CyberSchoolBus/untour/index.html*.

---

* Thomas G. Weiss, Tatiana Carayannis, Louis Emmerij, and Richard Jolly,
  UN Voices. Bloomington, Ind.: Indiana University Press, 2005, p, 171.

(continued from page 31)
invasion of Finland), it reluctantly accepted a compromise. If
the vote concerned a *substantive* matter (rather than a simple
procedural one), like imposing economic or military sanctions,
then any one of the permanent members could stop council
action (including against itself). In other words, on substantive
matters, it would take only one of the permanent members to
paralyze the entire council.

As this decision would dictate the entire future course of
the UN's ability to respond to global threats, it is important to

ask why the framers embraced such an unwieldy voting plan for the council? Nearly all UN observers agree that without such a pressure valve, neither the Soviet Union nor the United States would have joined the United Nations, dooming it to fail from the start. Moreover, there was a concern that if the major powers could not prevent enforcement action against themselves, as Japan, Germany, Italy, and the Soviet Union were unable to do during the league era, some of the biggest players in the international system would sit outside of the world forum, rendering the United Nations meaningless.

With a fragile consensus achieved among the Allied powers about the overall framework of the organization, the United Nations Conference opened in San Francisco on April 25, 1945. Still a few weeks before Germany's May 8 surrender and several months before Japan's, 282 official delegates from 51 countries, supported by 2,400 staff personnel, convened on the West Coast of the United States to finalize the terms of the new organization. Unlike the secret deliberations of the Paris conference in 1919, the meeting was conducted in an extraordinary glare of publicity. There were 2,600 radio and print reporters and hundreds of concerned private citizens in attendance. Many of the meetings were in fact open to the public.

The new UN Charter, with its 111 articles, was signed by all participating states on June 26, 1945. The final result borrowed heavily from the experience of the League of Nations, but it also reflected new realities and visions of the post-World War II landscape. For the charter to become a reality, all five permanent members of the Security Council had to approve it, as well as a majority of the other signatories. The United States was the first to do so, on July 25, 1945, by a vote of 89 to 2. By October 24, the required number and combination of countries had ratified the charter, making that day celebrated annually as United Nations Day.

Until its permanent headquarters could be built, the UN General Assembly met in London. The first meeting took place on January 11, 1946. The mood, according to a report in the *Times of London*, was jubilant and enthusiastic. As the article exclaimed: "The welfare of every one of us is bound up with the welfare of the world as a whole, and we are all members one of another."[5]

OPTIMISM TURNS TO DISAPPOINTMENT: TWO SUPERPOWERS TRY TO RUN THE SHOW

When the UN opened for business, 51 countries were the original members. The name *United Nations* was initially the designation of the World War II Allied coalition, and to be eligible as a founding member, a country had to have declared war against the Axis by March 1, 1945. Thus, early membership was denied to the defeated enemy powers, including Germany, Japan, and Italy. Moreover, vast parts of the globe, particularly in Africa, the Middle East, and southern Asia, were still under the control of European colonial powers, although colonialism's clock was ticking.

The United States emerged from the war comparatively unscathed, and found itself, for the first time in its history, an economic and military powerhouse. Most of the original UN-member governments were highly indebted to the United States for its support during the war, giving Washington the upper diplomatic hand in the new organization. President Roosevelt, who had unexpectedly passed away in the war's closing months, had originally envisioned that the United States and the Soviet Union would remain as united in peace as during the war. However the two began to clash even before World War II's guns had barely quieted. Within two years of the UN's launch, the Cold War erupted. The two superpowers, as they became known, carved the world—and the new organization—into two competing blocs.

Since the 1917 Bolshevik Revolution, the Soviet Union espoused a belief that the world's ills stemmed from the capitalist and free-market economic principles advocated by the

Western European countries and the United States. It was not until after World War II, however, that the USSR was at the top of the global power pyramid along with the United States. As of 1945, Moscow was in a position to spread its version of Communism, advocating single-party rule and state-owned economies, to other countries. The United States, however, desired to see a world of representative democracies and free-market economies and sought to "contain" the Soviets.

Washington and Moscow attempted to best one another around the world diplomatically, economically, and militarily, in a geo-strategic chess game. The conflict was called the "Cold War" (rather than "hot") because it never became a shooting war between the two countries themselves. Instead the superpowers' mutual hostility was channeled through other countries' wars. If this political rivalry did not make matters tense enough, both countries were the first to develop nuclear weapons (the United States in 1945 and the USSR in 1949), a potentially catastrophic military capability unparalleled in human history. The world feared that any flash point between the two in any part of the globe could spiral into nuclear annihilation.

So almost from its birth, until nearly 50 years later, the United Nations was another game board for the Americans and the Soviets. The new UN Security Council's success hinged upon postwar cooperation between the two. Yet each superpower now possessed a single blocking veto as a result of earlier wartime political compromises. The young council, the central forum tasked with managing international crises, was instantly paralyzed.

Washington and Moscow could not even agree as to who could be the newest members of the UN, since potential candidates had to be nominated first by the Security Council. Only nine countries, not closely identified with either camp, were able to join in the first five years of the UN's existence, and none in the next five. In 1952 alone, 21 countries unsuccess-

Because the Cold War caused so much friction between the United States and the USSR, the UN became the stage for Soviet–American political tensions. As the threat of nuclear war loomed over the world, civil defense organizations created posters (like the one above), booklets, songs, and public service announcements to educate the public in case of nuclear attack.

fully applied for admission. Finally in 1955, during a thaw in the relations between the United States and the Soviet Union (following the death of the Soviet's longtime leader Joseph Stalin), a "package deal" was concluded that allowed 16 states to enter simultaneously.

While the entrance process was easier for the majority of the applicants after 1955, the Cold War's lingering impact on UN membership remained significant. The superpower contest had split Germany into East and West Germany, Vietnam into North and South Vietnam, and Korea into North and South Korea, in a Communist/non-Communist pattern known as divided states. The two Germanys did not join the UN until 1973 (later merging as a single Federal Republic of Germany in 1990). Following the end of the Vietnam War, a unified Vietnam entered in 1977. North and South Korea were finally permitted to join the UN only as two separate states in 1991, as the Soviet Union was collapsing.

A different Cold War-era membership controversy that still endures has been the representation of China at the UN. During World War II, a nationalist, American-supported government was in control, but for two decades prior to that conflict, the nationalists had been embroiled in a brutal civil war with the Communists. It was the pro-Washington nationalists that accordingly controlled China's member-ship in the UN, and most significantly, one of the Security Council vetoes when the UN began in 1945. By 1949, this major Washington ally was overthrown by the Chinese Communist movement. The Nationalist government fled to Taiwan, an island off the coast.

In the "you're either with us or against us" mentality of the Cold War, what would now happen with the China seat in the UN? Would the United States keep a pivotal ally on the Security Council or would the Soviets finally gain a friend in that forum? Because China was already a member, the question centered upon which government should be recognized rather than if a country could join. And as government recognition rather than state member admission was the issue, the charter dictated that the matter move into the UN General Assembly for consideration.

Through extraordinary parliamentary maneuvering in the Assembly in the 1950s and 1960s, a forum where the United States could still count on a sympathetic majority, the United States managed to keep the Communists on mainland China (known as the People's Republic of China, or PRC), with the world's largest population, from securing its UN seat for over 20 years! A Soviet-Chinese Communist rift, however, emerged in the late 1960s. The United States politically capitalized on this falling-out between the world's two largest Communist countries by dropping its recognition of the government on Taiwan as the sole representative of the Chinese people (a key PRC demand) and recognizing the PRC instead in 1972. The UN General Assembly followed accordingly, recognizing the PRC as the legitimate representative of the Chinese people the same year. Since 1971, Taiwan (Republic of China, or ROC) has sat outside of the UN.

STRENGTH IN NUMBERS?
THE GLOBAL SOUTH TRIES TO TAKE OVER

While the UN experienced one major membership fault line immediately after it started in the 1940s, another one began to open by the 1960s. Yet unlike the superpower rift, the impact of this divide upon UN functions remains significant. Rather than the ideological East-West competition, the UN was now encountering a new clash in perspectives between North and South.

Starting in the 1950s, vast swaths of the world's population, many for centuries under colonial control, began to demand their independence. After the 1955 package deal, membership grew from 76 members to 110 by 1962, the growth almost exclusively due to the successful African and Asian independence movements.

By the late 1960s, an emerging membership pattern at the United Nations became strikingly clear. These newly independent countries, when joined by their Latin American counterparts, whom mostly had become independent a century earlier, were now becoming the majority of the UN's members. Riding the strength of their combined numbers, these countries ushered in a completely different political, and particularly economic, vision of the world. They became collectively known as the Global South. The Global South consists of countries that are largely (although not exclusively) concentrated south of the equator and who have experienced colonial rule. They are economically less developed or undeveloped, and they face difficulties consistently providing their citizens with adequate levels of nutrition, health, and education. The Global North refers to the world's wealthier and more industrialized countries, situated primarily to the north of the equator. Many are former colonial powers.

Not surprisingly, the Global South demanded that the UN promote a distinctively different vision from that of the United States and its wealthier supporters. By 1964, these new members organized themselves into a formal bloc known as the Group of 77 (later to grow to more than 100 but retaining the same name). They now make up three-quarters of the UN's current membership. The Global South calls on the Global North to reform the international playing field so that it is fairer to the Global South and seeks a more equitable distribution of the world's wealth to ease the gap between the economic "haves" and "have-nots."

The East-West confrontation, lead by the Soviet Union and the United States, wreaked its greatest havoc on the UN Security Council, where each could wield their veto to frustrate what the other superpower wanted. However the impact of the Global North-Global South divide was most evident in the UN General Assembly. The assembly, where every country has an equal vote, no matter what its size or power, means that those countries that can muster a majority will dominate. Since the 1960s, the Global South has ruled the UN General Assembly.

GETTING A SECOND CHANCE: THE UN AND THE END OF THE COLD WAR

By 1991, the international political system had experienced a startling transformation. In December of that year, the Soviet Union had disintegrated and no longer legally existed. This astonishing development was the final chapter of an unfolding two-year drama whereby Soviet political and military presence in Eastern Europe had been ejected, Germany became reunified for the first time in more than 40 years, and the Soviet Union itself had jettisoned Communism as its governing ideology. The Cold War was now over.

For an organization so heavily crippled by the hostility between the United States and the Soviet Union almost since its birth in 1945, the end of the superpower contest gave the UN a new lease on life. One reflection of the UN's rejuvenation was the remarkable surge in membership it has experienced since the early 1990s. Membership expanded from 159 in 1990 to its current roster of 192 by 2006 (Montenegro was the 192nd). Seventeen new members alone resulted from the collapse of both the Soviet Union and another large, multinational Communist state, Yugoslavia (Russia would assume the place of the former Soviet Union, including the council permanent seat). Several other first-time entrants during this period, however, were states that had been in existence for hundreds of years. Many microstates like Liechtenstein, San Marino, and Andorra, which had remained aloof from international relations for centuries, decided they could no longer afford to remain outside of the UN in a highly interdependent world. Similarly, historically neutral Switzerland, after years of popular referendums rejecting UN membership, also decided

After WWII ended, Germany was split in half, between democratic West Germany and USSR-backed East Germany. In addition, the city of Berlin, located deep in the heart of East Germany, was similarly divided. In order to prevent East Germans from escaping to the West, the Communist government closed down the border, and Berliners awoke one morning in 1961 to find a large wall running through their city. The two sides of Germany joined the UN in 1973, and later, after the wall fell in 1989, reconnected and became a member under one unified name.

to join in 2002. UN membership, for the first time in its history, is nearly universal.

One membership issue remains stubbornly unresolved. Starting in 1991, the Republic of China, or Taiwan, sought entrance into the UN as a separate state from that of the People's Republic of China. Since the Communist government in Beijing believes that the island and people of Taiwan should be reincorporated as part of the People's Republic, the PRC now wields its mighty Security Council veto to freeze Taiwan out of the organization. In 2007, Taiwan's government began petitioning the UN General Assembly and the UN Secretariat to be accepted as a UN member under the name "Taiwan." This new official designation would completely disassociate the island from its powerful mainland neighbor. In a statement before the opening of the 2007 General Assembly, however, Secretary-General Ban Ki-moon stated it was not legally possible to accept Taiwan's bid, leaving the island's government and people in an international legal limbo.

How the UN Works

. . . [T]here is no such single thing as the UN.[6]

—Nancy Soderberg, former U.S. ambassador
to the United Nations

WHAT DOES IT REALLY MEAN WHEN NEWSPAPER HEADLINES blare "The United Nations has voted to . . ." or "The UN has failed . . . " or "Government X is taking the matter to the United Nations"? The reality is that the UN is actually a sprawling global network of six main organs and dozens of committees, specialized agencies, programs, and commissions that support the organization's initiatives in nearly every aspect of human concern. All of these bodies have their own

The United Nations System
Principal Organs

Trusteeship Council

Security Council

General Assembly

Subsidiary Bodies
Main committees
Human Rights Council
Other sessional committees
Standing committees and
ad hoc bodies
Other subsidiary organs

Advisory Subsidiary Body
United Nations
Peacebuilding Commission

Economic and Social Council

Functional Commissions
Commissions on:
 Narcotic Drugs
 Crime Prevention and
 Criminal Justice
 Science and Technology for
 Development
 Sustainable Development
 Status of Women
Population and Development
Commission for Social
 Development
Statistical Commission

Regional Commissions
Economic Commission for
 Africa (ECA)
Economic Commission for
 Europe (ECE)
Economic Commission for Latin
 America and the Caribbean
 (ECLAC)
Economic and Social Commission
 for Asia and the Pacific (ESCAP)
Economic and Social Commission
 for Western Asia (ESCWA)

Other Bodies
Permanent Forum on
 Indigenous Issues (PFII)
United Nations Forum on Forests
Sessional and standing
 committees
Expert, ad hoc, and related bodies

Related Organizations
WTO World Trade Organization
IAEA International Atomic
 Energy Agency
CTBTO Prep.Com PrepCom for
 the Nuclear-Test-Ban-Treaty
 Organization
OPCW Organization for the
 Prohibition of Chemical
 Weapons

International Court of Justice

Specialized Agencies
ILO International Labor
 Organization
FAO Food and Agriculture
 Organization of the
 United Nations
UNESCO United Nations
 Educational, Scientific and
 Cultural Organization
WHO World Health Organization
World Bank Group
IBRD International Bank
 for Reconstruction and
 Development
IDA International Development
 Association
IFC International Finance
 Corporation
MIGA Multilateral Investment
 Guarantee Agency
ICSID International Center for
 Settlement of Investment
 Disputes
IMF International Monetary Fund
ICAO International Civil Aviation
 Organization
IMO International Maritime
 Organization
ITU International
 Telecommunication Union
UPU Universal Postal Union
WMO World Meteorological
 Organization
WIPO World Intellectual
 Property Organization
IFAD International Fund for
 Agricultural Development
UNIDO United Nations Industrial
 Development Organization
UNWTO World Tourism
 Organization

Secretariat

Departments and Offices
OSG Office of the
 Secretary-General
OIOS Office of Internal Oversight
 Services
OLA Office of Legal Affairs
DPA Department of Political Affairs
DDA Department for
 Disarmament Affairs
DPKO Department of
 Peacekeeping Operations
OCHA Office for the Coordination
 of Humanitarian Affairs
DESA Department of Economic
 and Social Affairs
DGACM Department for General
 Assembly and Conference
 Management
DPI Department of Public
 Information
DM Department of Management
OHRLLS Office of the High
 Representative for the Least
 Developed Countries, Landlocked
 Developing Countries and Small
 Island Developing States
DSS Department of Safety and
 Security
UNODC United Nations Office on
 Drugs and Crime

UNOG UN Office at Geneva
UNOV UN Office at Vienna
UNON UN Office at Nairobi

© Infobase Publishing

Subsidiary Bodies
Military Staff Committee
Standing Committee and
ad hoc bodies
International Criminal Tribunal for
the former Yugoslavia (ICTY)
International Criminal Tribunal
for Rwanda (ICTR)
UN Monitoring, Verification
and Inspection Commission
(Iraq) (UNMOVIC)
United Nations
Compensation Commission
Peacekeeping Operations
and Missions

Programs and Funds
UNCTAD United Nations
Conference on Trade and
Development
 ITC International Trade
 Center (UNCTAD/WTO)
UNDCP United Nations Drug
Control Program
UNEP United Nations
Environment Program
UNICEF United Nations
Children's Fund

UNDP United Nations
Development Program
 UNIFEM United Nations
 Development Fund
 for Women
 UNV United Nations Volunteers
UNCDF United Nations Capital
Development Fund
UNFPA United Nations
Population Fund
UNHCR Office of the United
Nations High Commissioner
for Refugees

WFP World Food Program
UNRWA United Nations Relief
and Works Agency for
Palestine Refugees in
the Near East
UN-HABITAT United Nations
Human Settlements Program

Research and Training Institutes
UNICRI United Nations
Interregional Crime and
Justice Research Institute
UNITAR United Nations Institute
for Training and Research

UNRISD United Nations
Research Institute for
Social Development
UNIDIR United Nations Institute
for Disarmament Research

INSTRAW International
Research and Training
Institute for the
Advancement of Women

Other UN Entities
OHCHR Office of the United Nations
High Commissioner for Human Rights
UNOPS United Nations Office
for Project Services

UNU United Nations University

UNSSC United Nations System Staff College

UNAIDS Joint United Nations Program on HIV/AIDS

Other UN Trust Funds
UNFIP United Nations Fund for International Partnerships   **UNDEF** United Nations Democracy Fund

Note: Solid lines from a principal organ indicate a direct reporting relationship; dashes indicate a nonsubsidiary relationship.

distinct powers, processes, and political challenges. Journalist Linda Fasulo refers to the system as the "UN village" consisting of different neighborhoods, each possessing its own unique and special character. Some are select and exclusive, like the 15-member Security Council, with a small group of diplomats who work intensely together on a daily basis. Yet there is also "that other part of town, the General Assembly, where crowds of ordinary nations mill about, shouting and waving their hands."[7]

Therefore when one hears: "The United Nations . . . " it is always first necessary to ask, which part of the United Nations? The UN, as laid out in the charter, has six principal parts. They include the General Assembly (UNGA); the Security Council (UNSC); the Secretariat headed by the secretary-general (UNSG); the Economic and Social Council (ECOSOC); the International Court of Justice (ICJ); and the Trusteeship Council. Only after understanding each body's operating context can global citizens fully appreciate the UN's balance sheet of successes and failures.

Despite the tens of thousands of people affiliated in one way or another with the UN, the member countries and those working for it are all guided by the seven basic "house rules" or operating principles that are laid out in the charter's Chapter 1, Article II. After 60 years, it is the first five that still remain particularly important. In summary, the members:

1. are considered equal in the organization, no matter what their geographic or population size or amount of power;
2. will take the rules seriously when joining the organization;
3. should try to work things out peacefully if they have differences with one another;
4. should not threaten violence or actually physically hurt one another;
5. agree to do what they can to help the United Nations if the organization decides to take action.

ALL STATES ARE LEGALLY CREATED EQUAL: THE UN GENERAL ASSEMBLY

"The United Nations Has Passed the United Nations Declaration on the Rights of Indigenous Peoples." . . . "The United Nations Has Renewed Financing for the UN Mission in Sierra Leone." . . . "The World's Leaders Came to Address the Opening of the United Nations." . . . "The United Nations Holds a Special Session on Climate Change." Declarations, financing, summits, and special sessions are all the purview of the UN General Assembly (UNGA).

Structure and Voting

The UNGA is a plenary body, which means that all members of the organization belong to it. Because overall UN membership is currently at 192, the assembly also has 192 members. It is the only forum in the entire UN decision-making system that has this universal representation, leading some to refer to it as an "international parliament." Every assembly member state has one vote, regardless of its power, population, or wealth. Most decisions are made based on the simple majority rule of 51 percent or more to pass.

The UNGA meets yearly as a plenary body, starting on the third Tuesday in September for a period of three months. At the UN's fiftieth anniversary in 1995, the world's leaders (rather than ambassadors) represented their countries at the assembly opening for the first time. Their appearance at the start of the UNGA's session has now become an annual tradition. Once the plenary concludes in early January, the members break out into six committees to focus on specific agenda items assigned to them by the larger assembly. It can also meet for special sessions to highlight a theme of concern (children, HIV/AIDs) or an emergency session in response to a peace and security concern (such as the Israeli-Palestinian conflict).

Power and Responsibilities

The UNGA is the world's town hall, its central discussion forum. While at first glance, the assembly's charter powers "to consider," "to weigh," and "to deliberate" appear not to be very commanding, the assembly is in fact the world community's central catalyst for new global policies. Although UNGA resolutions do not require UN members to do anything per se (in other words, they do not carry the force of law), successfully passed resolutions reflect the general will of the international community to initiate cooperation in a particular area, such as poverty reduction, environmental protection, health, education, or human rights.

Many UNGA resolutions will evolve into binding legal agreements, or treaties, in later years. One of the most famous is the UNGA resolution containing the 1948 Universal Declaration of Human Rights (UDHR). The UDHR is the most quoted international legal document after the UN Charter itself and set into motion an entire wave of landmark human rights treaties, including the International Civil and Political Rights Covenant and the International Economic, Social and Cultural Rights Covenant, both of which are in force. Later UNGA resolutions led to the International Criminal Court's establishment and treaties on climate change and biodiversity. Recent resolutions are laying the groundwork for new agreements in such diverse issue areas as rights of persons with disabilities, nuclear terrorism, organized crime, human cloning, and child prostitution and pornography.

The assembly has several internal administrative functions. The UNGA has sole control over the UN budget. It also elects the Security Council's non-permanent members as well as the ECOSOC's. Upon the nomination of the Security Council, it appoints the secretary-general and approves new UN members and co-selects (along with the UNSC) International Court of Justice judges.

How the General Assembly Really Works

One major flash point continues to be the UN budget, which the assembly exclusively controls. The United States has only one of 192 votes to approve the budget, but it is responsible for 22 percent of it. In fact the eight richest countries pay for approximately 75 percent of the budget, yet only have eight votes among them. Meanwhile the majority of the UN, which is extremely poor, jointly contributes only a small part of the remaining 25 percent. Many Americans, including some past U.S. presidents and members of Congress, have been critical of the size of the American budget assessment. On occasion, Washington has withheld its contribution in protest, plunging the UN deeper into debt. But Timothy Wirth, president of the United Nations Foundation, urges everyone to take into account the "multiplier effect."

> It is far cheaper for the United States and other nations to share the costs and burdens of international security than it is to go it alone. Most U.S. taxpayer dollars spent through the United Nations and other major multi-lateral institutions are leveraged four-fold or more. So when the [United States] puts 25 cents towards a UN project, the rest of the world generally adds in 75 cents. . . . Cooperation with the UN is a bargain.[8]

Recent reform efforts have also aimed at improving the efficiency of assembly operations. Its critics believe that too much time is wasted during each session and that better scheduling is needed, redundant speeches should be eliminated through the use of joint statements, and committee work should be organized better. With 192 countries all wanting to have their say on any given issue, it is a challenge, particularly given that the assembly is influenced by the will and priorities of shifting parliamentary majorities. At the beginning, the United States and its supporters easily shaped what the UNGA discussed

The Group of Eight (G8) is an international forum for the governments of Japan, Canada, France, Russia, Germany, the United States, the United Kingdom, and Italy (represented here by their respective leaders, along with the EU Commission president, *end right*). The countries that make up the G8 represent only 14 percent of the world's population, but account for about 60 percent of the world's economic output. Constructed to be informal, it lacks an official administrative structure like those for international organizations such as the UN and the World Bank.

and decided. Starting in the 1960s, with the emergence of the new Global South that included the poorer countries of Africa, Asia, and Latin America, the voting tide turned. At that point the United States became frustrated that it could not direct the course of the UNGA.

However, with the end the Cold War, these fault lines are not quite what they used to be. Now, an extraordinary 75 percent of UN General Assembly resolutions are unanimous. Former U.S. ambassador to the UN John Negroponte captures the tough deliberations that surround the assembly's special sessions:

Nerves can get frayed and you have these marathon meetings that go on until eight in the morning, and you have NGOs in the bleachers which are pushing single-minded positions. But even there, particularly if you can succeed in achieving consensus, if you can reach consensus on a document, I think there's always a huge sense of relief even amongst those who were opposed to positions we had. They can say to themselves, at least we produced something at the end of this.[9]

Botswana's former ambassador to the UN, Joseph Legwaila, provides a slightly different perspective: "Some people had almost come to believe the Security Council, plus perhaps key agencies like UNICEF and UNDP [UN Development Program] were the UN and that the General Assembly counted for nothing. But those of us from the developing countries are in charge there. The General Assembly may be a talking shop, but it is a universal and a very necessary one."[10]

ALL STATES ARE NOT CREATED EQUAL IN TERMS OF POWER: THE UN SECURITY COUNCIL

"The United Nations Votes to Impose Another Round of Economic Sanctions upon Iran." . . . "The United Nations Deadlocks in Responding to the Myanmar Crackdown." . . . "The United Nations Authorizes Peacekeeping Mission for Sudan." Many of the world's thorniest challenges related to peace and security land first at the UN Security Council for consideration, making this among the most visible and public of all the UN's main organs.

Structure and Voting

The UNSC has 15 members total. The five permanent members (referred to as the "Perm 5" or "P-5") never rotate off the council. They are China (PRC since 1971), France, Russia (USSR from 1946–1991), the United Kingdom, and the United States. There are also 10 temporary members, who serve two-year, staggered terms (meaning five go off each year). They are elected by the UNGA from its membership and the seats are distributed according to a regional formula from the late 1960s. The allocations are as follows: 5 from Asia/Africa; 2 from Latin America; 1 from Eastern Europe; 2 from Western Europe, and "other" (Australia, Canada, etc.).

In 2007–2008, the non-permanent seats were held by the following countries: Belgium, Congo, Ghana, Indonesia, Italy, Panama, Peru, Qatar, Slovakia, and South Africa. Competition to be one of the regional picks is highly intense. Within a few years of becoming independent from the former Yugoslavia, Slovenia decided to run for one of the two seats representing Eastern Europe in 1998–1999. Danilo Turk, Slovenia's first ambassador to the United Nations, recalled that Slovenia's successful bid brought significant exposure to his new country: "We discovered that half of what was important internationally about Slovenia related to the Security Council in those two years. For a small country, this is an incredible exposure."[11] Ambassador Turk also believed that while the permanent five countries attract much of the world's attention, the smaller temporary members have a very key role to play:

> If a country like Slovenia fails, it is no problem, but if a big country fails with a proposal, that usually has political repercussions. So small countries, non-permanent members, can be constructive and genuinely helpful members of the Security Council. They can afford some imagination and experimentation. I always believed that. I never thought that only permanent members count.[12]

The council has two voting formulas. On procedural matters, the vote for successful passage is at least 9 of the 15 members. Regarding those items deemed substantive (see below under "Powers and Responsibilities"), the vote is also 9 of 15, but in addition all permanent five members must agree. In other words, if only *one* of the permanent members (China, France, Russia, the United Kingdom, or the United States) registers a negative vote, then the measure fails. This ability of just one of five to block all Security Council action is known as a great power veto. Abstentions by the permanent five do not stop a vote from passing. If the permanent members agree but four of the temporary members do not, the measure also fails. The fact that the temporary members can block a resolution desired by all five permanent members is sometimes referred to as the "sixth veto."

Unlike the General Assembly, which meets three months of the year, the council is deemed to be in permanent session, and in no case can go longer than two weeks without meeting. The UNSC president (the position rotates monthly among its 15 members) can call a meeting or the assembly or the secretary-general may refer a matter to the body.

Powers and Responsibilities

The council is the central UN organ responsible for the maintenance of international peace and security. It is the only UN body whose resolutions have the force of law upon the UN member states. It may investigate disputes, recommend peaceful methods of settlement, and call for a variety of sanctions (diplomatic, economic, military) against an identified aggressor. Such measures are considered substantive matters for the purpose of voting. The UNSC also nominates member countries for admission and secretary-general candidates to the General Assembly for approval. Both nominations are subject to the substantive voting process. It also co-selects ICJ judges with the assembly.

How the Security Council Really Works

The wielding of the veto by the five permanent council members explains nearly every United Nations failure or success in responding to international crises since its creation in 1945. As the UN's birth coincided with the dawning of the Cold War, the feuding United States (and its allies) and the USSR paralyzed the council with their respective vetoes from the outset. As the United States could also rely in the early years on its friends, both among the permanent members, including China (Taiwan), France, and the United Kingdom, as well as among the temporary members (since the assembly was also dominated by Washington's supporters), the USSR was particularly isolated. This is reflected in the fact that between 1946 and 1969, the Soviet Union registered 105 vetoes while the United States cast none! However once the United States-France-United Kingdom alliance began to fray by the late 1960s, and temporary members from a changing assembly began to produce more independent-minded members, the United States began to use its veto, starting in 1970.

The end of the Cold War by 1991 meant an exciting new era of cooperation for the council, with an unprecedented flurry of passed resolutions authorizing a wide variety of peace activities, including dispute resolution measures and authorization of peacekeeping and enforcement. The final release of the Cold War's grip on the functioning of the UNSC has prompted many to state that the UN was actually born starting in 1991 rather than 1945.

Viewing it another way, the U.S. State Department Web site on United Nations voting practices shows the extraordinary increase post-1991 in the number of council meetings held as well as the resolutions that were considered and adopted.

This new spirit of harmony has not meant that the permanent five has agreed on everything since the early 1990s. While the era of two camps has disappeared, each permanent

UN SECURITY COUNCIL VOTING PRACTICES

YEAR	COUNCIL MEETINGS	RESOLUTIONS CONSIDERED	RESOLUTIONS ADOPTED
2006	273	89	87
2005	235	71	71
2004	216	62	59
2003	208	69	67
2002	238	70	68
2001	192	54	52
2000	167	52	50
1999	124	67	65
1998	116	73	73
1997	117	57	54
1996	114	59	57
1995	130	67	66
1994	160	78	77
1993	171	95	93
1992	129	74	74
1991	53	42	42

member still has vested interests, and many of the proposals never even make it to the council table as proposed resolutions. The majority of UNSC business is actually conducted outside of the public eye in "off the record sessions." This style reduces the amount of political grandstanding in front of the cameras, which the council is sometimes famous for.

China, for instance, has significant trade ties to Sudan, so it has been hesitant to respond aggressively to the dire humanitarian situation in Darfur. If the dispute under consideration involves parties with diplomatic relations with Taiwan, Beijing will also wield its veto. The Russians are reluctant to support the admission of Kosovo as a new member, as Kosovo is attempting to secede from longtime Russian ally Serbia. The United States continues to bloc UNSC consideration of Israel related to its conflict with the Palestinians. When the United States could not obtain Security Council support among the other four permanent members for its Iraq military plans in the spring of 2003, Washington simply moved ahead on its own. Significant numbers of vetoes have also been used to block nominations of new UN members as well as secretary-general candidates, as the United States did so famously with the failed reappointment of Boutros Boutros-Ghali in 1996.

This ability of just five countries to stop the global response machinery to security threats has prompted strong calls for Security Council reform. At its heart, the reform discussion revolves around the concern that the Security Council is controlled by a World War II victorious allied coalition. Japan and Germany, defeated more than 60 years ago during World War II and the second and third largest contributors to the UN budget, have been shut out unless they rotate on as temporary members. There are rising powers, including Brazil, India, and South Africa. It is generally agreed that the current permanent members will not surrender their veto power, and granting it to other countries will only bring further gridlock. Therefore, most of the reforms have focused upon potentially expanding the council to 21 to 25 members and recognizing other countries, such as those mentioned above, as permanent members with no veto power. Who gets to be on the council, however, is politically sensitive and much of the reform requires amendments to the charter. All of the permanent five must approve them!

THE WORLD'S CIVIL SERVICE: THE SECRETARIAT AND THE SECRETARY-GENERAL

"We were dealing with actual human beings, and I could put my head to the pillow at night knowing that what I did made a real difference in people's lives—people I could see and feel and meet and touch and actually talk to."[13] This is how Shashi Tharoor, whose home country is India, described his work for the UN High Commissioner for Refugees (UNHCR). The UNHCR is one part of the vast UN Secretariat, the organization's administrative backbone. Mr. Tharoor began his UN career by working at UNHCR in 1978, and he later worked for other parts of the secretariat, including in peacekeeping operations, within the secretary-general's office and ultimately became the undersecretary-general for Communications and Public Information. Many who work for the secretariat stay there for their entire professional careers, passionate about making a difference in the world.

Structure

The secretariat consists of 9,000 international civil servants based primarily at the UN's New York headquarters but also at UN satellite offices in Geneva, Switzerland; Nairobi, Kenya; and Vienna, Austria. Adopting the practice of its league predecessor, secretariat employees do not serve the interests of their home countries but rather the principles and objectives of the UN organization. They also represent the sweeping diversity of the membership itself.

At the top of the secretariat is the secretary-general (UNSG), who is nominated (subject to the permanent five veto) by the Security Council and approved by the General Assembly. There have been eight UN secretaries-general. The current one, Ban Ki-moon, a South Korean, assumed office in January 2007. Secretaries-general serve five-year terms with the potential for renewal.

Powers and Responsibilities

The secretariat is where the day-to-day activities are carried out by administrative personnel dealing with all of the world's challenges, from literacy to nuclear proliferation. The secretariat consists of technical experts, medical professionals, economic advisers, military specialists, and educators. It is also where the UN's public relations staff, accountants, document librarians, administrative assistants, translators, housekeepers, groundskeepers, and tour guides also work.

(continues on page 62)

THE CEO OF THE WORLD

"My experience, each morning, may not be unlike yours. We pick up our newspapers or turn on the TV—in New York, Lagos, or Jakarta—and peruse a daily digest of human suffering. Lebanon. Darfur. Somalia. Of course, as Secretary-General of the United Nations, I at least am in a position to try to do something about these tragedies. And I do, every day."* This was Secretary-General Ban Ki-moon's description of his position after his first five months in office. Yet he also agreed with the words of the first secretary-general, Trygve Lie, that the secretary-general's post is "the most impossible job on this earth."**

Ban began his term as the eighth UN secretary-general in January 2007. A native of South Korea, he holds an undergraduate

(continues)

Former secretary-general Kofi Annan and his successor, Ban Ki-moon

(continued)

degree in international relations from Seoul National University and a master's degree in public administration from Harvard. In addition to Korean, he is fluent in English and French. Secretary-General Ban has dedicated his entire career to public service, serving in his home country's diplomatic corps in a variety of capacities, including several postings at the UN. He was South Korea's foreign minister when he was picked for the UN's top job. In his acceptance speech upon his appointment in October 2006, the incoming secretary-general described his feeling of profound connection to the organization: "It has been a long journey from my youth in war-torn and destitute Korea to this rostrum and these awesome responsibilities. I could make the journey because the UN was with my people in our darkest days. It gave us hope and sustenance, security and dignity. It showed us a better way. So I feel at home today, however many miles and years I have traveled."[***]

During his first year in office, Secretary-General Ban has established his own leadership approach of arguably one of the most important bureaucracies in the world. His personal style is modest, preferring to negotiate quietly and build consensus behind closed doors. However Ban is also an active world traveler, not only visiting important capitals but also places to which he wants to draw the world's attention. He was the first secretary-general, for instance, to visit Antarctica, to highlight global warming's devastating impact there.

Mr. Ban has a tough act to follow. His predecessor, Kofi Annan of Ghana, is considered one of the greatest secretaries-general that the institution has ever had. Serving from 1997 to 2006, Mr. Annan was the first to be promoted from within the Secretariat ranks itself, starting his UN tenure in 1962 with the World Health Organization and serving as Undersecretary-General for Peacekeeping when he was appointed to the highest position.

Annan combined an insider's view of the organization; a sensitivity to the potential and plight of his home continent of Africa; a strong personal charm; astute political skills; and a constant vision that the UN, in the end, represented individual people. While still in office, he explained it this way: "I sometimes say things in my speeches and statements, knowing that it will help those without voice. They can quote the Secretary-General, 'As the Secretary-General said'—and they will not go to jail.... I give them voice by putting my thoughts and ideas in a way that they can quote.... I have not hesitated to speak out. I know not everybody likes it, but it is something that has to be done...."†

In 2001, the Nobel Peace Prize was awarded to Kofi Annan and the UN. The Nobel Committee cited Annan's attempts to modernize the UN bureaucracy and make it more responsive to emergencies; his prominent peacemaking role in a variety of disputes throughout the world, ranging from East Timor to Kosovo; and his advance of causes like human rights, HIV/AIDS, and the environment, among many others. In the words of Nobel Chair Gunnar Berge, "No one has done more than Kofi Annan to revitalise the UN." ††

---

  * "Why the World Has Changed in the UN's Favor," *Newsweek International*, 4 June 2007. Available online at *http://www.un.org/sg/press_article.shtml*.

 ** Ibid.

*** "Acceptance Speech by H.E. Mr. Ban Ki-moon on Appointment as the 8th Secretary-General of the United Nations," 13 October 2006. Available online at *http://www.unsgselection.org/files/BankiMoon_AcceptanceSpeech_13Oct06.pdf*.

 † Thomas G. Weiss, Tatiana Carayannis, Louis Emmerij, and Richard Jolly, *UN Voices: The Struggle for Development and Social Justice*. Bloomington, Ind.: Indiana University Press, 2005, p. 357.

†† "Presentation Speech by Gunnar Berge, Chairman of the Norwegian Nobel Committee," 10 December 2001. Available online at: *http://www.nobelprize.org/nobel_prizes/peace/laureates/2001/presentation-speech.html*.

(continued from page 58)

Besides being the chief administrative officer of the entire secretariat and the public face of the UN, the secretary-general fulfills a number of other important roles. The secretary-general is the chief diplomat, and he frequently offers his services as a neutral mediator in conflicts involving member states. He is empowered to bring matters to the attention of the Security Council and often works to achieve a consensus among the permanent five on peace and security matters. The UNSG, along with the secretariat, proposes agenda items and new strategic directions for consideration by the rest of the UN bodies. The previous secretary-general, Kofi Annan of Ghana, attempted to focus the world body's attention on internal organizational reform, to the many challenges and promises of the African continent, and in 2000 he presented the landmark Millennium Report, encouraging a renewed focus on the environment, HIV/AIDS, and education, among other pressing issues.

How the Secretariat Really Works

The size and efficiency of the secretariat have been heavily debated for many years. Depending on who is asked, the UN bureaucracy is either vastly bloated and wasteful or woefully understaffed and underfunded. One of the loudest critics was the United States, the largest contributor to the UN budget throughout the 1980s and early 1990s. Bureaucratic reforms in 1997 led to Secretariat employees being reduced by 25 percent from 12,000 to 9,000.

Because of the selection process that requires approval of all five UNSC permanent members, none of the secretaries-general have ever been from the great powers. Those holding this important position have come from traditionally middle or smaller powers that are politically neutral or nonaligned. While no official geographic quota system is in place, world regions over the course of the UN's existence have clamored for their opportunity to have a candidate from their part of the world. Past secretaries-general (all male) include:

Trygve Lie	Norway	1946–1952
Dag Hammarskjöld	Sweden	1953–1961[*]
		(killed while in service)
U Thant	Burma	1961–1971
Kurt Waldheim	Austria	1972–1982
Javier Perez de Cuellar	Peru	1982–1992
Boutros Boutros-Ghali	Egypt	1992–1996
Kofi Annan	Ghana	1997–2006
Ban Ki-moon	South Korea	2007–

On paper, the secretary-general appears to be an incredibly powerful person, the "president of the world" in some respects. To be effective, the person who holds this office must be guided by a strict sense of impartiality in addressing the needs of 192 member countries. As Boutros Boutros-Ghali explains: "If one word above all is to characterize the role of the Secretary-General, it is independence. The holder of this office must never be seen as acting out of fear, or in an attempt to curry favor with, one state or a group of states. . . ."[14] Kofi Annan agrees, to a point: "Impartiality does not—and must not—mean neutrality in the face of evil. It means strict and unbiased adherence to the principles of the Charter."[15]

Yet the reality is that the secretary-general must always work within the boundaries of what the international community of governments, and particularly the great powers, will allow him to do. He may use the force of his individual personality, his personal ability to persuade and motivate others, including the global public, to support his agenda. However he risks alienating member states, and particularly the permanent five, at his own peril. This was a painful lesson learned in 1996 by Boutros Boutros-Ghali, the very energetic secretary-general following the end of the Cold War. The United States, put off by Boutros-Ghali's activism (including some harsh criticism of Washington), vetoed his candidacy for a second term. Boutros-Ghali is the only secretary-general to be denied a renewal in UN history.

WHEN JUDGES RESPOND TO INTERNATIONAL CONFLICT: THE INTERNATIONAL COURT OF JUSTICE

At the first sitting of the International Court of Justice (ICJ) in 1946, the General Assembly's first president, Paul Henri Spaak, discussed the quiet but significant role of the ICJ: "I would not venture to assert that the Court is the most important organ of the United Nations; but I think I may say that in any case there is none more important. Perhaps the General Assembly is more numerous; perhaps the Security Council is more spectacular. . . Your work will perhaps be less in view, but I am convinced that it is of quite exceptional importance."[16] Far from the commotion of UN headquarters in New York, where the other five main UN bodies reside, the ICJ meets in The Hague, Netherlands, to bring international law to bear upon some of the world's most intractable conflicts.

Structure and Voting

The World Court consists of 15 judges from around the world. The Security Council and the General Assembly co-select the justices. They serve nine-year terms (renewable). By tradition, five of the judgeships are always allocated to the permanent member countries of the UN Security Council. Also similar to the Security Council, the rest of the seats are distributed along regional lines, with three from Africa, two from Latin America, two from Asia, two from Western Europe and other (Canada, Australia, and New Zealand) and one from Eastern Europe. No country may have more than one judge on the Court sitting at the same time.

Sir Robert Jennings, president of the court from 1991 to 1994, describes the judges' strong commitment to international law despite the considerable diversity among them: "The judges are from many different parts of the world . . . from different cultures, and not least from very different legal systems. The layman's question is always the same: How do you manage to have a coherent and useful deliberation in those circumstances? . . . The answer is that in practice the problem hardly arises. . . . International law is a language which transcends different tongues, cultures, races and religions."[17]

The court decides cases by a majority vote, with a minimum (a quorum) of nine needed to render a decision. Court decisions are final, meaning that they cannot be appealed.

Powers and Responsibilities

The main purpose behind the ICJ is to serve as a court of law for the countries of the international community. When governments have disputes with one another, they are able to use the court to peacefully resolve the conflict through the application of international law. Only states can sue or be sued in the court. The ICJ cannot be used by private citizens, interest groups, or businesses (although they may convince their home government to sue another country on their behalf). At the request of the General Assembly, the Security Council, or other UN bodies, the ICJ may also render an advisory opinion concerning points of international law.

How the ICJ Really Works

In a community where the members recognize no higher legal authority above themselves, as in the case of the world's sovereign states, the power of the ICJ is very different from that of courts within countries. The UN recognizes governments' sensitivity regarding sovereignty through a provision in the ICJ Statute (attached to the UN Charter) known as "the optional clause." By accepting the ICJ Statute's Article 36, countries can opt to accept the compulsory or automatic jurisdiction of the court. This acceptance means that if a country is sued by another country at the ICJ that has also

The International Court of Justice is another way to promote peaceful resolutions of conflicts between countries, before it escalates into more serious actions. In 2007, President Rosalyn Higgins, seen here, announced the verdict in a longtime case on ocean territory between Honduras and Nicaragua.

accepted compulsory jurisdiction, the country will automatically appear before the court. A little more than 60 UN member states have accepted Article 36. If a country does not accept compulsory jurisdiction, it does not mean that it will not go to court if sued. It merely means that the government can pick and choose. For example, the United States has not accepted the ICJ's compulsory jurisdiction since 1988. When Mexico sued the United States, however, over the failure of local police to notify Mexican citizens of their right to contact their home government following arrest within the States, the United States went to the ICJ as a defendant. Washington lost the case in 2004, and President Bush announced the United States' acceptance of the verdict.

Compared to domestic courts, the ICJ is used far less frequently. Since its inception, it has heard on average 12 or fewer cases a year, although the end of the Cold War has witnessed an upturn in its work. The reasons for its weaker usage are many. From the outset, the number of eligible parties is only 192. Going to the ICJ is also a highly time-consuming and expensive process, as some complicated cases can take years to have a decision rendered. For governments who feel a sense of urgency or for poorer countries, the ICJ is not always a viable option.

The ICJ, however, still remains the central legal hub for the world community. As veteran international legal analyst Shabtai Rosenne explains: "The cases before the Court have related to vast areas of our planet . . . the Court has had to deal with cases involving the lives and the well-being of huge numbers of men and women."[18] For some countries, going to the court is part of an ongoing set of negotiations. Just like with individuals in the United States, a smaller country might bring attention to a cause by publicly suing. Surprisingly, countries with friendly relations also use the court (as in the case of the United States and Mexico), as a way of isolating one irritant in otherwise amicable relations. Moreover, the rate of compliance by states with the decisions handed by the ICJ is exceedingly high.

PEACE IS NOT JUST ABOUT GUNS: THE ROLE OF THE ECONOMIC AND SOCIAL COUNCIL

". . . [T]he role of ECOSOC is vital in giving people food, shelter, and clothing, and to see to it that they get education, health, and job opportunities. Why then does it not catch the public's imagination? The answer is that the work is just too complex, too multi-faceted, too varied. It's a story that the media can never hope to capture in one quick news-bite" writes UN observer Wilfred Grey.[19] ECOSOC is the hub of an expansive array of commissions, specialized agencies, and nongovernmental organizations, all dedicated to world peace achieved through alleviating global poverty and its related social ills.

Structure and Voting

The Economic and Social Council consists of 54 members, who are elected by the General Assembly and serve three-year terms. Like the assembly, the majority of ECOSOC members are poorer. The United States and other wealthier powers, however, are guaranteed seats as they represent the potential donors to realize ECOSOC's projects. Allocations are as follows: 14 African states, 11 Asian, 6 Eastern European, 10 Latin American and Caribbean, and 13 Western European and "other." The committee meets twice a year, holding one session in New York and the other in Geneva, Switzerland.

ECOSOC also oversees five regional commissions and nine functional commissions that focus on particular issue areas, such as human rights, narcotic drugs, sustainable development, and population.

Powers and Responsibilities

While ECOSOC is one of the six principal bodies of the UN and therefore implies equality of status, it actually reports to the Assembly on a wide array of quality of life matters, ranging from human rights to transportation, from culture to poverty, and from science to narcotics trafficking. It is tasked with conducting research studies and reports on economic and social conditions, and it is considered to be the global leader regarding statistical data related to these two areas.

ECOSOC also plays a coordinating role. It oversees the 14 UN Specialized Agencies (World Health Organization, World Bank, International Monetary Fund, etc.) and the dozen UN program and funds, including UN Environment

Program, World Food Program and UN Population Fund. Nongovernmental organizations, or private citizens' groups, also gain access to the UN system after being recognized by the ECOSOC through the granting of "consultative status."

How the ECOSOC Really Works

From one perspective, the ECOSOC appears to be powerful in that it is the hub of activity that involves nearly 70 percent of the UN system's financial and human resources. On the other hand, the ECOSOC reports to the UN General Assembly. It therefore does not have final authority on economic and social matters.

Despite the charter's intent that the ECOSOC be the focal point for all UN-related economic and social activity, the rapid proliferation of affiliated organizations, programs, and funds further weakens the council's ability to coordinate efforts. Characterizing the relationship between the ECOSOC and the UN Specialized Agencies, Brian Urquhart and Erskine Childers wrote: "The orchestra pays minimum heed to its conductor."[20]

A VICTIM OF ITS OWN SUCCESS: THE TRUSTEESHIP COUNCIL

The Trusteeship Council was created to promote the decolonization process in the international community after World War II. It oversaw the transition of 11 "trust territories" from that of colonial holdings to independent states. Following the achievement of independence by the Pacific island territory of Palau in November 1994, the last trust territory, the council ceased operations. It is slated to be eliminated as a principal organ of the UN when the charter is revised. The Trusteeship Council's success in helping move nearly a dozen colonies to self-governance is considered one of the greatest triumphs of the UN.

For anyone interested in "sitting in" on any of the meetings of the various UN bodies, it is possible to hear daily live Web casts, including those of the Security Council and the General Assembly, at http://www.un.org/webcast/.

A Global 911?:
Peace, Security,
and the UN

The nations and peoples of the United Nations are fortu-nate in a way that those of the League of Nations were not. We have been given a second chance to create the world of our Charter that they were denied. With the Cold War ended we have drawn back from the brink of confron-tation that threatened the world and, too often, paralyzed our Organization.[21]

—**Former secretary-general Boutros Boutros-Ghali,**
in *Agenda for Peace*

ON AUGUST 2, 1990, THE COUNTRY OF IRAQ, UNDER THE dictatorship of Saddam Hussein, invaded its tiny southern neighbor Kuwait. The invasion by one UN member of a fellow

UN member was not, unfortunately, an isolated incident. Despite the charter's clear legal prohibition against the use of aggressive force among its members, several such incursions had occurred in the post–World War II era, including those committed by the Security Council's permanent members.

On the other hand, what happened at the UN after the invasion was out of the ordinary. On the very day that the attack began, the matter came immediately before the UN Security Council. Just two years earlier, the council most likely would have deadlocked due to the USSR's strong relationship with Iraq, and the long-term American support of Kuwait and neighboring Saudi Arabia. In Security Council Resolution 660, however, 14 council members (Yemen abstained), including all five permanent members, agreed to strongly condemns the Iraqi invasion and demanded an immediate and unconditional withdrawal.

Yet that was just the beginning. In the following months, the council passed 10 more resolutions, many of them 15 to 0, increasing the diplomatic and economic pressure upon Iraq. Finally, on November 29, 1990, the council passed Resolution 678, authorizing "member states cooperating with the government of Kuwait" to use "all necessary means" against Iraq if it did not withdraw from Kuwait by January 15, 1991. "All necessary means" opened the door for a collective military response, which is permitted according to the UN Charter.

For only the second time in its history, UN members engaged in a joint military action. The first time, in Korea in 1950, was a quirk of history related to the Soviets' Council boycott over the UN not recognizing Communist China. The 1990 response was therefore truly historic and ushered in a new era of council activism in the area of peace maintenance.

These renewed opportunities notwithstanding, the fact that the council was not able to halt the genocide in Bosnia and Rwanda in the 1990s or prevent or respond to the spring

When Saddam Hussein's Iraq invaded neighboring Kuwait in 1990, the UN responded to this offense with a united, strong condemnation of the action. It was the first time the countries had worked so quickly and agreeably in the organization's history. Later, when the Security Council authorized military action from member states against Iraq *(above)*, it signaled a new, more active role for the UN and its efforts to maintain peace.

2003 United States invasion of Iraq, and struggles to halt the humanitarian suffering in places as disparate as Sudan and Myanmar (Burma) currently, shows that the "Global 911" system is far from perfect.

The international response mechanism to peace and security challenges is flawed for a variety of reasons. First, as the focal point for global peace maintenance among the world's states is the Security Council, any action is subject to the individual permanent five veto, which protects the national interests of China, France, Russia, the United Kingdom, the United States, and their respective allies. UN action, therefore, is inconsistent and prone to significant political bargaining among the major powers, rather than resulting in a neutral and impartial response. Second, because countries are legally and politically sovereign, even a highly determined UN may have a tough time getting a government to do what the organization wants. Governments can be even more stubborn than individual people, and in a sovereign state system, one cannot call the police in, because there is no international police that has power over them. Nor can countries be forced to go to court if they do not want to. These two considerations taken together—the nature of Security Council decision making and national sovereignty—profoundly shape UN successes and challenges in the areas of peacemaking, peacekeeping, and peace enforcement.

PEACEMAKING:
THE BEST PLACE TO START AND END

When rifts arise between UN members, the organization's automatic first response is to attempt to solve the disagreement peacefully or through what is also known as "pacific settlement." This approach remains the top priority throughout a dispute's life cycle. Military force is never considered as a first or even a final option in most cases. This international community ethic is even enshrined in the charter's Article 2 principles that "All members shall settle their international disputes by peaceful means. . . ." The charter's Chapter 6, Article 33 identifies the majority of the methods that are applied. They include:

Negotiation: Direct discussion of a dispute between the diplomatic representatives of involved parties. Negotiating is the only process that does not include a "third party," meaning an impartial actor not related to the dispute.

Enquiry (or Inquiry): If the parties cannot agree even on the basic facts underlying the disagreement, then a third party can be sent to investigate in hopes of lessening tension and finding a rational solution.

Mediation: Also a third-party technique whereby an outside actor recommends how a conflict might be resolved, although the mediator's proposals do not have to be accepted.

Conciliation: A formal commission that makes nonbinding (free to accept or reject) recommendations regarding a dispute.

Arbitration: A dispute is submitted to a panel of arbitrators that have been previously chosen by the parties. The sides agree in advance that they will accept the arbitration panel's decision as final and binding. There is a Permanent Court of Arbitration located in the Netherlands, but many parties also create temporary arbitration panels just for their specific issue.

Judicial settlement: The International Court of Justice will review a dispute between countries, based on international legal principles. Like arbitration, ICJ decisions are also binding, although decisions are nearly impossible to enforce.

Good offices: This mechanism is not included in Article 33, but is a heavily used technique by the UN secretary-general and his special envoys. Good offices are offered when the parties involved will not speak to each other directly. The secretary-general or his representatives can serve as a communication go-between to get discussions started.

While these techniques were employed throughout the UN's existence, the Security Council's application of them surged with the end of the Cold War in the early 1990s. This was particularly evident regarding civil wars, the most common form of violence in the post-World War II period. Burundi, Cambodia, El Salvador, Guatemala, Mozambique, Namibia, Sierra Leone, and Sudan (between its north and south) are just a few examples where pacific settlements of disputes have been achieved.

PEACEKEEPING:
A LITTLE HELP FROM UN FRIENDS

One technique that the United Nations has utilized to great success is the sending of peacekeeping missions. The peacekeeping concept does not appear anywhere in the UN Charter, nor did it exist at the time of the League of Nations. Early in the UN's existence, however, it became clear that peacemaking between parties could be greatly helped along by a neutral and nonfighting military presence standing between the parties while the necessary trust building took place.

The mission's neutrality is important to emphasize, because unlike the military troops deployed under a peace enforcement action, as in Korea in 1950 and Iraq in 1990, these military forces aren't dispatched against an identified enemy. Rather the troops are there to help foster the peacemaking process between parties. Peacekeepers arrive only with the consent of the parties involved, are minimally armed, and their weapons may be used only in self-defense (so that they don't end up becoming involved in the fray).

Almost from the beginning, the UN sent peacekeepers to some of the tensest hot spots of the immediate post–World War period, including Greece, the Kashmir border between India and Pakistan, and Palestine. Troops performed a number of essential functions, including cease-fire monitoring, patrolling borders, observing troop withdrawals, and generally serving as a buffer between disputing parties. Although these activities were vital for keeping the peace, the Cold War's paralyzing effect on the Security Council meant that only 17 missions were authorized during the entire period between 1947 and 1988.

The year 1989 marked a dramatic turning point for peacekeeping, both in their number and the kind of activities that fell under the umbrella term of peacekeeping. With the easing of tension between the United States and USSR, the Security Council authorized more missions during the five-year period between 1989 and 1993 than it had going back the previous 40 years! No longer limited to being buffers or observers, peace-keepers also now deliver electoral assistance and humanitarian aid, demobilize armed groups, clear land mines, help rebuild a country's infrastructure, engage in human rights monitoring, and serve as a local police force, in addition to the already long list of their previous responsibilities.

The 1989 United Nations Transition Assistance Group (UNTAG) mission for Namibia marked peacekeepers' first of many electoral assistance efforts in the post–Cold War era. As Namibia prepared for its long-sought-after independence, its authorities held elections for its new Constituent Assembly. UN peacekeepers fanned out across the country to help with electoral tutorials and monitor the process so that Namibian citizens did not feel intimidated by Namibia's former ruler, South Africa, and its secret police, when they went to vote. Matthew Lunga recalls his very first vote at the age of 45:

> I got up before dawn and walked down to the polling station, thinking that I would be the first one in line. But to my surprise, there were dozens and dozens of people already lined up. It took hours before I could put my ballot in the box. It was getting so hot under the sun, I thought the woman behind me, who was carrying a baby in her arms, would faint. But she just kept on smiling. I asked her: "Are you all right?" She smiled again and she replied: "I can vote!"[22]

Although the original superpower rivalry no longer impedes the use of peacekeeping, there are still a number of issues. Even though the Security Council may reach a decision to authorize a mission, it does not mean that it will actually happen. Once a mission is approved, the secretary-general has to go to the UN member states and ask them to contribute troops. Depending on the complexity of the mission, the commitment of one of the major military forces is usually needed

(continues on page 80)

THE ALL-FEMALE PEACEKEEPING UNIT

In January 2007, a new peacekeeping unit arrived to help the people of Liberia. This West African country is still recovering from a brutal civil war that raged between 1989 and 2003 and killed 250,000. The police contingent, sent by India, was deployed to join the larger UN Mission to Liberia (UNMIL) peacekeeping force, with the intent of doing what the UN does best, helping the country rebuild.

However this particular unit was a first for the UN. India's troop contribution was the UN's first all-female unit. The 103 members are highly experienced policewomen who have served in difficult locations in their home country, including the troubled region of Kashmir. They were competitively selected to serve in this historic mission and had to pass rigorous physical tests. In India, all-female units are common.

The arrival of the all-female force was one of the first tangible signs of a new UN strategy of enhanced female participation in peacekeeping, peacemaking, and peace-building efforts. In October 2000, the Security Council adopted Resolution 1325 that stressed the importance of sensitivity to gender in all aspects of UN peace initiatives. The Security Council's action came on the heels of a greater understanding of war's unique toll on women. According to the landmark study *Women, Peace and Security*, "Women and girls are often viewed as bearers of cultural identity and thus become prime targets. Gender-based and sexual violence have increasingly become weapons of warfare and are one of the defining character-istics of contemporary armed conflict."* The report mentions rape, sexual slavery, and the intentional transmission of HIV/AIDS as several of the wartime techniques in evidence.

This ugly fact is why the all-female peacekeeping unit was greeted so enthusiastically in the Liberian capital of Monrovia. During the Liberian civil war, an estimated 40 percent of all Liberian females were raped, and even now sexual assault is the most widespread serious crime in the country. Female peacekeepers are considered less intimidating to traumatized women and children. Sexual assault victims may also feel more comfortable reporting it to other women. As Unit Commander Seema Dhundia

(continues)

(continued)

expressed: "Seeing women in strong positions, I hope, will reduce the violence against women."[**]

The Liberian government also hopes that Liberian women will consider joining its national police force as a career, resulting in "gender mainstreaming" of the national units too. Commander Dhundia has the same wish: "Women see us out on the streets every day putting on uniforms, carrying heavy [weapons], and performing our duties. . . . It will definitely get them inspired and motivated to come forward."[***]

Early indicators show that Liberian women have come out in greater numbers to join the national force. The government is certainly enthusiastic about the mission and its aims. Liberia's president is Ellen Johnson-Sirleaf. President Johnson-Sirleaf is Africa's first elected female head of state.

---

[*] *Women, Peace and Security: Study Submitted by the Secretary-General Pursuant to Security Council Resolution 1325 (2000)*. New York: United Nations, 2002, p. 2. Available online at *http://www.unicef.org/emerg/files/wps.pdf*.

[**] Tristan McConnell, "All-Female Unit Keeps Peace in Liberia," *PeaceWomen.Org*. Available online at *http://www.peacewomen.org/un/pkwatch/News/07/LiberianfemPKERS.html*.

[***] Ibid.

(continued from page 77)

to form the core, and other countries join in. Many smaller countries may be willing to lead, but may not be able to pull it off related to logistics, troop strength, or other considerations. Even if the secretary-general can make it happen, the government or other parties involved in the conflict may refuse at any time to give their consent to the mission being stationed on their territory. Once a mission is mobilized and arrives, peace-keepers face numerous challenges on the ground. Suddenly a force that may have a dozen nationalities must work together as an integrated whole.

Staying neutral is also a challenge. What if it is obvi-ous to the peacekeepers on the ground that one party being monitored is clearly the perpetrator and the other the vic-tim? This is what happened in Bosnia in the 1990s. In one of several infamous incidents, the UN had declared the town of Srebrenica as a safe haven to be protected by UN peacekeepers. In 1995, Bosnian Serb forces overwhelmed the primarily Muslim enclave. Dutch peacekeepers, completely outnumbered and lesser-armed, called for UN air support to repel the Serb offensive. It never materialized. UN officials worried that if the peacekeepers responded, its forces would be considered a party to the conflict and that its humani-tarian assistance efforts throughout Bosnia would be shut down. Moreover, the Serbs had the diplomatic support of the Russians on the Security Council. The Serbs would ulti-mately kill more than 8,000 Bosnian Muslims in what became known as the Srebrenica Massacre. In October 2007, Dutch peacekeeping veterans returned to the area to confront the trauma of what they had witnessed and were unable to stop. Monique Bergman was 20 when she served there: "Today I feel the same helplessness I felt in those days. . . . Not being able to do anything is a horrible feeling, which haunted me for years. For years I have been mentally ill because of what happened here."[23]

More than 2,300 peacekeepers have lost their lives in ser-vice to the UN. Still, despite the many risks and challenges, the world community's enthusiasm for peacekeeping is at an all-time high. The year 2006 was a record year for peacekeeping troop deployment, with 100,000 troops from a wide variety of small and middle powers participating in 18 missions deployed under the UN banner. While peacekeeping is an approach that

The UN peacekeepers have served countless people in conflicts around the world, and many have lost their lives. In memory and appreciation of Timorese peacekeepers who died during a peacekeeping operation in Timor-Leste, a staff member with the UN Integrated Mission in Timor-Leste (UNMIT) places a wreath at a memorial during a ceremony commemorating International Day of United Nations Peacekeepers on May 28, 2007.

is a relative newcomer to world affairs, it is now difficult to imagine successful peacemaking without it.

PEACE ENFORCEMENT: ALL FOR ONE AND ONE FOR ALL

Peacemaking and peacekeeping both start with the assumption that no side is to blame or is guilty. There are occasions, however, when the council deems that a certain member has violated the charter and that collective enforcement action is necessary. The idea that countries would band together in the event of a breach of peace was the primary motivation behind both the league's and UN's respective creations. Possible measures go by a variety of names, including "collective security," "peace enforcement," and "sanctions" (punishments). They are discussed in the charter's Chapter 7.

Even when there is a clear indication that a member country is a threat to peace or has acted aggressively, the UN's first response will not be with military force. On the contrary, the hope is that negotiation, mediation, and other means of peaceful settlement will do the trick. If not, the next steps are what are referred to as "nonmilitary sanctions." According to Article 42, these include the partial or full cutoff of economic, communication, transportation, or diplomatic ties between the international community and the offending country. If all of these tools fail, then Article 43 calls for "such action by air, sea, or land forces as may be necessary to maintain or restore international peace and security."

It is the Security Council that is empowered to determine what course of action should be taken and when to take it. This authority means that military action is never taken against one of the permanent members, even when they themselves have violated the charter. This design was intentional, so that the league experience of losing many of its great powers would not be repeated.

There have been only two instances where the UNSC has authorized collective military enforcement. They include the military response following the June 1950 North Korean invasion of South Korea and after the 1990 Iraqi attack of Kuwait. The first case may be surprising, given that the Soviets supported North Korea and the United States was allied with South Korea. The council should have deadlocked, as it frequently did. However the Soviets were actually boycotting the council at the time in protest that its new ally Communist China had not been allowed to assume the China seat (a mistake that

Moscow never made again!). If it had not been for that wrinkle, no collective military sanction would have taken place during the first nearly 50 years of the organization's existence.

The UN's military action against Iraq was much more along the lines envisioned by the charter framers. Three months after Iraq illegally entered Kuwait, and with Washington and Moscow diplomatically closer, the council agreed unanimously in November 1990 "to use all necessary means" to repel Iraq. An ultimately successful military counteroffensive was launched in January 1991 with 28 UN members participating, and a total of 675,000 troops (the United States contributed 425,000).

Even though Washington and Moscow no longer tussle on the council like they used to, collective military sanctions will continue to be rare. In both the Korean and Iraqi cases, there was a great power—the United States—with a vested interest in making it happen, including providing the bulk of the forces. But even more importantly, the nature of violence today is not as the international community originally perceived it in 1945. At the end of World War II, the worry was about international conflicts, with one country attacking another, and a clear, identifiable aggressor. However the loss of life today stems more from civil wars, and with more shadowy combatants, like terrorists and guerilla fighters, rather than recognizable government forces.

Nonmilitary collective measures, especially economic sanctions, are therefore more common. Economic sanctions are designed to deprive a state of the benefits of economic relations with the rest of the world. This approach is generally preferred as a supposedly nonviolent way to achieve a political objective, or in the case of the UNSC, compel a member country to abide by the charter. Economic sanctions are somewhat controversial. They are economically effective, in that they can devastate the targeted economy, but political success is another

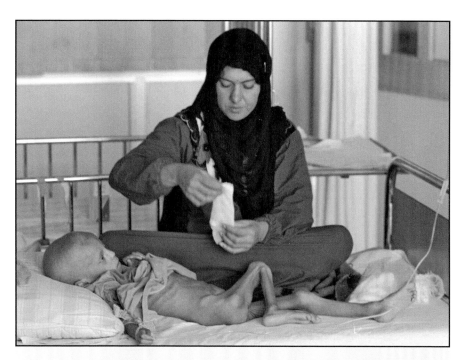

Economic sanctions are sometimes controversial because of their effect on the population. During the Iraq-Kuwait conflict, the UN placed sanctions on Iraq, which severely restricted its food resources and possibly resulted in the death and malnutrition of many Iraqi children.

matter. They can take years to achieve their political end, and it has emerged that full-scale sanctions, those that completely cut a country off from any economic interaction with the outside world, can still result in loss of life. This was startlingly apparent in Iraq, where perhaps hundreds of thousands of children are believed to have died because of malnutrition and poor health. This humanitarian catastrophe was partially due to the deteriorating economic situation caused by sanctions imposed starting in 1990 and continuing almost unabated through 2003, until the U.S. invasion. Now the UN focuses instead on the use of "smart sanctions" that target government officials rather than the general population.

A landmark 2005 study found that the number of armed conflicts around the world had fallen 40 percent since 1992. The number of what the report defined as the "deadliest" conflicts, costing more than 1,000 lives, had plunged by 80 percent. The researchers determined that three factors played a role, including the decolonization wave after World War II and, of course, the end of the Cold War. The third contributor was the UN, no longer paralyzed by the superpowers, dedicating new energy to peacemaking, peacekeeping, and sanctions initiatives.[24]

Peace Is Not Just About the Guns: Health, Wealth, and Human Rights

Today, in Afghanistan, a girl will be born. Her mother will hold her and feed her, comfort her and care for her just as any mother would anywhere in the world. In these most basic acts of human nature, humanity knows no divisions. But to be born a girl in today's Afghanistan is to begin life centuries away from the prosperity that one small part of humanity has achieved. It is to live under conditions that many of us in this hall would consider inhuman. Truly, it is as if it were a tale of two planets.

I speak of a girl in Afghanistan, but I might equally well have mentioned a baby boy or girl in Sierra Leone. No one today is unaware of this divide between the world's rich and poor. No one today can claim ignorance of the cost that this divide imposes on the poor and dispossessed who are no less deserving of human dignity, fundamental freedoms, security, food and education than any of us. The cost, however, is not borne by them alone. Ultimately, it is borne by all of us—North and South, rich and poor, men and women of all races and religions.[25]

—Secretary-General Kofi Annan,
2001 Nobel Peace Prize lecture

THERE IS A SAYING THAT "GEOGRAPHY IS DESTINY." IT MEANS that where one is born will shape a person's life. For a baby born in a country of the Global South, life may already be filled with extraordinary challenges from its first day on the planet. Chances are that if this child survives its first few days or even five years, it will not have enough food to maintain its own weight. He or she will grow up in a house that will literally be four walls made of something perhaps no stronger than cardboard. This child will have little access to schooling of any kind, and it's already predetermined that college is out of the question. No local doctors or even a nurse will be close enough to provide care. On average, if this child makes it into adulthood, it can expect to live to be around 58 years old. In the Global North, the same baby could expect to live to be 80 years old.

While in 1945, the UN founders placed the greatest emphasis on military security, they were aware that meeting the basic economic and social needs of the human family was also vital for the achievement of world peace. According to the charter's Chapter 9, Article 55, the organization is dedicated to economic and social cooperation "with a view to the creation of conditions of stability and well-being which are necessary for peaceful and friendly relations among nations. . . ." The charter also called for the UN to promote higher standards of living, full employment, economic and social development, health, and respect for human rights.

There have been many extraordinary developments related to meeting essential human needs since 1945, with many parts of the world's population becoming less poor, healthier, better educated, and with their basic rights more respected than ever before in history. Yet the stark picture is that at the start of the twenty-first century, vast swaths of the world's citizens are none of these things. Today, 1.1 *billion* people live on less than one dollar per day. Another 1.7 *billion* people live on between one and two dollars a day. They live in societies where adequate food, safe drinking water, sufficient educational opportunities, health care, and housing are dreams, not daily realities. Such a grim existence often leads to political instability and the trampling of peoples' fundamental rights.

The Security Council is frequently the body that captures the headlines and draws the public's eye to the UN. Yet the majority of the UN system, in partnership with nongovernmental organizations, is dedicated to easing the plight of the world's poor with all of its attendant stresses and consequences. Today the UN dedicates 80 percent of its budget to economic and social issues.

Without all of the world's citizens living in basic dignity, the world can never truly be safe. As former British prime minister Tony Blair put it: "One illusion has been shattered on September 11: that we can have the good life of the [Global North] irrespective of the state of the rest of the world. . . . The dragon's teeth are planted in the fertile soil of wrongs unrighted, of disputes left to fester for years, of failed states, of poverty and deprivation."[26]

THE QUEST FOR HUMAN DIGNITY, PART I: THE ERADICATION OF POVERTY

Most of the states of the Global South can be classified as less-developed countries (LDCs) or developing countries. With a majority of the world's people living in more than 100 countries that fall into this category, there are many variations among them. Yet social scientists Ziring, Riggs, and Plano have identified several core profile indicators of an LDC.[27]

LDCs are not only situated geographically to the south of the richer, developed countries in most cases, but the poorest are in southern latitudes where the physical landscapes make daily existence difficult, including tropical climates, mountains, or deserts. People who live in these countries are poor, with an average annual income of less than $370 a year. They eke out a daily existence by subsistence agriculture, meaning that any crops that are raised are only for their own consumption rather than for market purposes. Extraordinary time and effort produces very little yield, and results can easily be wiped out by disease, animals, and natural disasters. If the LDC exports anything at all, these items are usually what are referred to as "primary products," unprocessed goods that will be refined or manufactured elsewhere. These goods tend to generate little income and are highly susceptible to market forces, such as declining demand in the industrialized countries or market oversupply. Typical primary products from LDCs are agricultural products like coffee and cocoa beans, raw minerals, or lumber.

LDCs have exploding populations. Ninety-five percent of the world's population growth occurs in these countries. Death rates have fallen due to technological innovations (medicines, sanitation, etc.) but birthrates also remain high. Families are concerned that they need to have numerous children to ensure that a few survive. Consequently, dramatic population increases overwhelm the governments' and economies' ability to provide fundamental social services like health and education.

Many countries of the Global South are also former colonial territories. During centuries of rule, colonial powers instituted policies for the benefit of themselves with no regard for the political, economic, or social development of the indigenous inhabitants. The imperial powers had failed to invest in the infrastructure of their distant holdings beyond the minimum needed to send raw materials back home. Only one road would be constructed, for instance, to transport diamonds from an interior mine or coffee beans from a plantation to shipping ports on the coast. The colonial administrators also pitted various local groups against one another in a concept known as "divide and rule." This policy was famously applied by Belgium in Rwanda, where the minority Tutsi were given preferential treatment in education and jobs over the majority Hutus, sowing the early seeds of the 1994 genocide.

As a result, after many new states had achieved the dream of political independence, they were immediately confronted by an entirely new set of challenges. In addition to historical resentments that began to boil over between various groups now living together as fellow citizens in new countries, recently independent states also faced a future with negligible communication or transportation grids in place, little electricity or clean water available, and few hospitals or schools. Today, only 31 percent of the Global South's roads are paved, compared to 95 percent in the Global North. In terms of electric consumption measured in kilowatt-hours, LDCs consume 970 compared to 8, 693 hours in developed ones. In the poorer states, 28 people out of every 10,000 people have personal computers, while that number rises to 466 per 1,000 in the developed North.[28]

LDCs have high rates of illiteracy. In South Asia, Africa, and the Middle East, nearly 50 percent of adults are not able to read or write a simple sentence. Compare these rates with 5 percent in the industrialized countries. Those who live in the Global South additionally suffer from high rates of epidemic or contagious diseases. While there are many such diseases, the most devastating in recent years has been the HIV/AIDS

Lack of clean, fresh water can be connected to economic, social, and medical problems in developing countries. This basic need is often taken for granted by people who have regular access to it, but for many who suffer from droughts or war, water can be limited to whatever they can find. Here, women in rural India must fetch dirty water from a pond also used by animals, due to a government ration of water in response to a drought.

epidemic. Ninety percent of the new infections occur in the Global South, and 5,861 die each day in the regions that make up this category, compared to 56 a day in the Global North. Sub-Saharan Africa is particularly impacted, where three-quarters of the world's HIV infections occur and are the leading cause of death.

A wide variety of UN programs, including the Joint United Nations Program on HIV/AIDS (UNAIDS), the

UN Conference on Trade and Development (UNCTAD), UN Population Fund (UNPF), UN Development Program (UNDP), World Food Program (WFP), and the United Nations Children's Fund (UNICEF), as well as myriad related agencies, such as the Food and Agriculture Organization (FAO), World Health Organization (WHO), World Bank and International Monetary Fund (IMF), among many others, have all worked tirelessly in the past several decades to alleviate the suffering of the world's poorest.

The combined efforts of these many related UN actors, in partnership with private organizations of citizens, in concentrating money, human capital, and the latest technology, have reaped impressive results. During the first two UN Decades on Water (from 1981 to 2002), more than 2 billion people had access to safe drinking water for the first time ever. The UN International Fund for Agricultural Development has helped 250 million of the world's rural poor. The World Bank has provided funds for 9,500 development initiatives, lending $20 billion per year. The Global Polio Eradication Initiative has been so successful that polio has been wiped out in 125 counties, and continues to plague only six, saving 5 million children from crippling paralysis. Smallpox has been completely eradicated from the planet. Child mortality rates, defined as under age five, have dropped to record low levels, declining from 13 million a year in 1990, to 9.7 million in 2007.

Statistics sometimes do not capture the human face of these successes. A village woman in northern Vietnam explains how her life and those around her were transformed as a result of the work of the UNDP and the FAO:

When we were growing rice we could never produce enough food and had very little cash income. I persuaded my family to take up aquaculture so that the children would have fish to eat. After I was invited to attend the training programme sponsored by UNDP and FAO, I took responsibility for our family's pond. Applying the techniques that I learned, we were able to harvest 400 kilograms of fish last year. This gave us more protein in our diet, as well as $330 from the sale of surplus fish. We used the money to buy livestock, repair the house, purchase furniture, pay fees for the children's education and our parents' health care—and restock the pond. Now I am teaching other women in the community to raise fish.[29]

While these accomplishments are impressive, the stubborn challenge of extreme poverty remains. The painful reality is that while children's mortality rates have indeed fallen, nearly 10 million children are still dying each year. During a historic gathering of the world's leaders at the 2000 opening of the General Assembly, Secretary-General Kofi Annan, inspired by the turn of the millennium, laid out eight goals to end extreme poverty with all of its related human costs. They became known as the Millennium Development Goals (MDGs) and they centered on a target date of 2015. They include:

Goal 1: Eradicate Extreme Poverty and Hunger
Goal 2: Achieve Universal Primary Education
Goal 3: Promote Gender Equality and Empower
         Women
Goal 4: Reduce Child Mortality
Goal 5: Improve Maternal Health
Goal 6: Combat HIV/AIDS, Malaria, and Other
         Diseases
Goal 7: Ensure Environmental Sustainability
         (including safe drinking water)
Goal 8: Build a Global Partnership for Development

In the secretary-general's 2005 progress report, Kofi Annan reported mixed progress related to the MDGs. Global poverty rates had fallen, as a result of economic growth in Asia. Many sub-Saharan African countries, however, had slid into even more dire economic straits. Universal primary education was close to being achieved in several developing regions, but again, fewer than two-thirds of southern African children were enrolled. Mortality (death) rates in children under the age of five had dropped, but 30,000 children were still dying every day from treatable diseases. HIV/AIDS, malaria, and tuberculosis continue to devastate large swaths of the population.

Part of the issue is that one year after the MDGs were announced, the United States experienced the September 11 attacks. This dramatically shifted the foreign affairs priorities of one of the major players at the UN, and the UN itself found its own policy attention divided. For many, meeting the Millennium Goals and the "war on terror" are part and parcel of the same policy agenda. The link between the despair caused by poverty and the prevalence of terrorism worldwide is undeniable.

THE QUEST FOR HUMAN DIGNITY, PART II: THE RISE OF HUMAN RIGHTS

As visionary as the League of Nations was, there was one notable—and intentional—omission: the promotion of human rights as one of its purposes. The governments after World War I simply could not come to a consensus that there should be international standards for the way people are treated. A state could abuse or deny its citizens, because it was sovereign.

World War II changed all of that. The atrocities of the Holocaust, the awakening of the colonies, the active roles played by U.S. President Franklin Roosevelt and his wife, Eleanor, all sparked a dramatic worldwide push to protect these rights for all human beings, regardless of where they lived. The UN Charter reflects this incredible change of heart. In the opening preamble, the organization's founding document declares the UN's determination "to reaffirm the faith in fundamental human rights, in the dignity and worth of the human person, in the equal rights of men and women. . . ." Article 1 states that the UN will promote and encourage "respect for human rights and fundamental freedoms for all without distinction to race, sex, language, or religion. . . . "

From the start, the UN has been at the forefront of efforts to recognize human rights for all. Within just a few years of its birth, the UN General Assembly passed the landmark Universal Declaration of Human Rights (UDHR) in December 1948. The UDHR is a comprehensive statement, acknowledging the broad spectrum of rights, ranging from political (free speech, freedom to worship) to economic and social (right to a job, right to health care) that different governments view as important.

The General Assembly endorsed it overwhelmingly, although as a nonbinding UNGA recommendation, it did not obligate its members to do anything. The vote hid the reality that while there was a growing consensus that human rights were important, what *kind* of rights should be protected was another matter altogether. For many countries, like the United States, it was most important to prevent the government from treating its citizens in an arbitrary way, particularly when it came to individual civil liberties. The United States and like-minded governments were concerned with rights that protected freedom of speech and expression, the ability to worship freely, not to be subject to arbitrary arrest, or be deprived of a trial. For other states, particularly Communist and Socialist govern-ments, what mattered more was that states provide a certain level of economic and social dignity. They wanted to see protec-tions related to housing, jobs, education, and health insurance. Accordingly, while the international community was developing a consensus about the need internationally and legally to recog-nize human rights, an agreement on what their actual content should be was far less attainable.

Nevertheless, despite its non-obligatory quality, the Universal Declaration is viewed as one of most important global statements regarding human rights, and it is the most quoted international document after the UN Charter itself. And since then, two binding treaties have entered into force, somewhat reflecting the international community's divide regarding the essential nature of human rights. These agreements are the International Covenant on Civil and Political Rights (ICCPR) and the International Covenant on Economic, Social and Cultural Rights (ICESC). Seventy-five percent of the world's countries have become parties to both, which is significant. Those among the remaining 25 percent, however, are also notable. The United States has steadfastly refused to recognize the ICESC and China the same with the ICCPR. The governments of both argue that the rights contained in the different documents are not fundamental in their respective societies.

More than 80 other single-issue agreements, including prohibition of genocide, racism, discrimination against women, and torture have also been fostered under the UN's aegis. Even children have been singled out in the 1989 Convention on the Rights of the Child. This global agreement covers the essential rights of children, related to economic exploitation and safe working conditions, sexual exploitation, physical or mental violence, and protection against family separation. Two more recent additions, or protocols, address child trafficking, prostitution, and pornography in one, and the other concerns children in armed conflict.

The recognition of such rights has been a major advancement, given the League of Nations' silence on the matter. The world is now keenly aware that there are transnational expectations for the treatment of human beings everywhere. Government compliance with international human rights standards remains a challenge in a global political system where sovereignty still holds sway. The organization Freedom House publishes annual reports on how well the world is

(continues on page 101)

THE TWELVE-YEAR-OLD SOLDIER

"I would like to give you a message. Please do your best to tell the world what is happening to us, the children. So that other children don't have to pass through this violence."* This was the plea of a former child soldier, a 15-year-old girl, who fled the Lord's Resistance Army in Uganda. It is difficult to imagine being a young teenager, barely out of childhood, and fighting in a war. Yet there are more than 300,000 children around the world in 30 countries, some as young as 9, who are categorized as "child soldiers." The Coalition to Stop the Use of Child Soldiers defines them as "any person under the age of 18 who is a member of or attached to government armed forces or any other regular or irregular armed force or armed political group, whether or not an armed conflict exists." These young people may actually fight or provide military support such as mine laying, spying, or transmitting messages. They may also serve as porters or domestic staff such as cooks, or be forced into sexual slavery.

When war occurs in an already poverty-stricken country, the social and economic fabric can completely unravel, and a family's already tenuous hold on survival weakens even more. Against this backdrop, society's youngest become increasingly vulnerable. Some are kidnapped and forced into military service. Others "voluntarily" join because no other options are available in their war-devastated communities where families and economies have collapsed and no employment or educational opportunities exist.

The occurrence of child soldiers is most concentrated on the African continent (100,000) but also exists throughout Asia, as well as in Russia (in Chechnya) and in Colombia. Currently in the United States, one of the most public faces of the child soldier tragedy is that of Ishmael Beah, whose autobiography, *A Long Way Gone: Memoirs of a Boy Soldier*, chronicles Beah's own traumatic experience in Sierra Leone's devastating civil war. He was just 12 years old in 1993 when

Young soldiers from a Congolese rebel movement group in January 2002.

rebels murdered his parents, and Beah began a wrenching three-year odyssey of survival, being forcibly recruited into the Sierra Leone army: "The villages that we captured and turned into our bases as we went along and the forests that we slept in became my home. My squad was my family, my gun was my provider and protector, and my rule was to kill or be killed. The extent of my thoughts didn't go much beyond that."** Beah eventually made his way to the United States, earning an undergraduate degree in political science at Oberlin College, and now lives and works in New York.

(continues)

(continued)

The UN system, particularly UNICEF, partners with numerous private child-advocacy groups to give hope to former young combatants. The approach known as DDR—Disarmament, Demobilization, and Reintegration—assists child soldiers returning to their homes. They are counseled regarding their past trauma and are also helped to build a positive future through education and job training.

Meanwhile, the UN continues to strengthen international human rights prohibitions against those parties that utilize children in their forces. In 2000, the Optional Protocol to Rights of the Child Convention on the Involvement of Children in Armed Conflict outlaws forced recruitment below the age of 18. The new International Criminal Court, whose statute makes it a war crime to conscript children under the age of 15, inaugurated its operations by indicting child-soldier recruiters in Uganda and the Democratic Republic of Congo. The Sierra Leone Tribunal is also currently trying former Liberian President Charles Taylor for a variety of crimes against humanity, including the use of child soldiers. As Ishmael Beah believes: "Given the circumstances, everyone is capable of it. It's part of our humanity to lose our humanity and also eventually to regain it."[***]

---

* Quoted in "Child Soldiers," Amnesty International homepage, *http://www.web.amnesty.org/pages/childsoldiers-index-eng*.

** Ishmael Beah, *A Long Way Gone: Memoirs of a Boy Soldier.* New York: Sarah Crichton Books, 2007, p. 126.

*** "War-torn Childhood 'A Long Way Gone,' but Not Forgotten," *USATODAY.com*, 14 February 2007, *http://www.usatoday.com/life/books/news/2007-02-14-beah-book_x.htm*.

(continued from page 97)

doing regarding human rights protections, particularly in the area of political freedoms. In its May 2007 report, "The Worst of the Worst: The World's Most Repressive Societies 2007," Freedom House surveyed 193 countries and 15 territories, such as Chechnya in Russia. The organization categorized 45 countries and 7 territories as "Not Free." Eight were particularly egregious: Burma, Cuba, Libya, North Korea, Somalia, Sudan, Turkmenistan, and Uzbekistan. As the report explains: "Within these entities, state control over daily life is pervasive and wide-ranging, independent organizations and political opposition are banned or suppressed, and fear of retribution for independent thought and action is part of daily life."[30]

The United Nations must work in tandem with thousands of international, regional, and national human rights groups made up of private citizens and supportive governments to continue to raise the bar. They have several shared goals. First, they work to build new protections into international law. Two new areas include the banning of a technology called cluster bombs, a single munition that drops several smaller bombs ("bomblets"), and to expand international humanitarian law to ensure that it not only protects civilians against inhumane conduct by national armed forces, but it also extends to private security contractors, like Blackwater in Iraq. Once international law is in place, the UN and its member governments work with human rights groups to monitor government compliance with established rights norms and to publicize concerns to the international community, in what is known as "name and shame." For instance, the International Committee of the Red Cross works with the UN to bring attention to the United States' treatment of detainees held at Guantanamo Bay, Cuba, according to the standards outlined in the 1949 Geneva Conventions. The Save Darfur organization has aggressively mobilized global public awareness of the Sudanese government's atrocities in the Darfur region in violation of the Genocide Convention. Amnesty International and Human Rights Watch are cooperating with the UN Secretariat regarding the Myanmar (Burmese) government's violent crackdown on pro-democracy protestors as protected by the International Covenant on Civil and Political Rights, the Torture Convention, and numerous other agreements.

For human rights supporters, one area that shows particularly exciting promise is the development of the International Criminal Court (ICC). After World War II, the victorious powers tried alleged German and Japanese war criminals. A proposal circulated at the new United Nations that a permanent war crimes court should be established to hold individuals responsible for crimes against humanity, including genocide. However the Cold War scuttled the plans. One former UN official said that "a person stands a better chance of being tried and judged for killing one human being than for killing 100,000."[31]

With the world a very different place by the 1990s, the UN Security Council began to authorize a number of ad hoc, or temporary, tribunals to hold individuals responsible for war crimes and crimes against humanity. They were established for the former Yugoslavia, Rwanda, and Sierra Leone. The first, the International Criminal Tribunal for the former Yugoslavia (ICTY), was truly historic in that it was the first court in history not to be associated with a victor, as those after World War II had been. The ICTY was established by the UN Security Council in 1993 and sits in The Hague, Netherlands. In Bosnia and other parts of the former Yugoslavia, more than 250,000 people were killed and more than a million were displaced. Through 2007, the ICTY concluded proceedings against 111 individuals, and proceedings continue against 50 more. One of the convicted, Dragan Obrenovic, stated after his plea agreement: "In Bosnia, a neighbor means more than a relative. In Bosnia, having coffee with your neighbor is a ritual, and this is what

The International Criminal Tribunal for the former Yugoslavia (ICTY), located in The Hague, has tried and convicted numerous individuals of genocide, war crimes, and crimes against humanity. Slobodan Milosevic, seen here on trial in 2001, was held responsible for the terror he orchestrated against others in the former Yugoslavia.

we trampled on and forgot. We lost ourselves in hatred and brutality. And in this vortex of terrible misfortune and horror, the horror of Srebrenica happened. . . . I will be happy if my testimony helps the families of the victims, if I can spare them having to testify again and relive the horrors and the pain during their testimony. It is my wish that my testimony should help prevent this ever happening again, not just in Bosnia, but anywhere in the world."[32]

Both the former Yugoslavia and Sierra Leone tribunals indicted the leaders of the respective countries, Slobodan Milosevic and Charles Taylor, for committing war crimes.

Holding a country's leader accountable for human rights violations was historically unprecedented. Milosevic died while in custody in 2006 of natural causes. Taylor's trial began in 2007.

This growing activity led to the establishment of a permanent court, the ICC, in 2002. It currently has 104 countries as parties to its statute. The United States has not become a party to the ICC. While much has been made of Republican President George Bush's administration's refusal to join, the fact is that the Democratic administration of President Bill Clinton was also highly reluctant and only signed the treaty (which still needed to be submitted for Senate approval) as he left office in December 2000. The most pressing concern for the United States is that of "politicized prosecutions," meaning that as an active global military power the United States will be vulnerable to infinite numbers of complaints that are more about political disagreements with American foreign policy than the achievement of justice. The ICC, participating governments, and human rights organizations insist that there are more than sufficient bureaucratic safeguards to prevent such a consequence from happening.

The ICC's 18 judges from around the world are empowered to hear cases related to genocide, war crimes, and crimes against humanity (including against current and former leaders). Its first arrest warrants were related to the brutal civil wars in Uganda and the Democratic Republic of the Congo. The ICC has recently issued indictments regarding atrocities committed in Sudan's Darfur region. The indictments include ministers in the Sudanese government.

The UN has successfully established a vision of a just world, whereby all of its citizens deserve to live in dignity, broadly defined. Combined with the efforts related to the Millennium Development Goals, there is a momentum to resolve some of the most pressing issues of humankind. Yet much remains to be done.

What If Earth
Is Sick?: The UN
and Environmental
Security

I started noticing a few years ago that some of my sheep were going blind. I thought it might be because of a virus. But the veterinarian told me that there was a big hole in the Earth's ozone layer. He said that ozone shields life on our planet from the sun's harmful ultraviolet radiation. This is really scary. What am I supposed to do? Have my sheep wear sunglasses, as many of our children now do? [33]

—Fernando Pinares, a sheepherder in Chile

IN APRIL 2007, THE UN SECURITY COUNCIL HELD A HISTORIC meeting. The body, charged with responding to threats to world peace, placed the issue of climate change on the agenda. It was the first time in the council's existence that the environment was being examined through the lens of security. The British foreign secretary Margaret Beckett, in placing the item on the UNSC schedule, queried: "What makes wars start? Fights over water. Changing patterns of rainfall. Fights over food production, land use . . . There are few greater potential threats to our economies, too . . . but also to peace and security itself."

No mention of the environment appears anywhere in the charter. The UN's founders believed that it fell under the scope of national governments and other organizations to address. The population was at 2.5 billion and mass industrialization had not yet taken off. However by the 1970s, international alarms began to sound, as a startling chain of events led to grave concerns about the planet's overall health. Skyrocketing population rates (it took just *12* years to go from 5 to 6 billion people) led to exploding consumption of natural resources, including water. Out-of-control consumption also results in extraordinary waste, polluting Earth and its atmosphere.

The UN realized it could no longer leave the matter to individual countries alone. If the environment is ill, then the human family will be jeopardized as much as by shooting wars. In 1972, the first UN conference in history dedicated to the environment was held in Stockholm, Sweden. This meeting was a starting point for promoting global awareness of environmental damage and sparked the creation of the UN Environment Program, the global hub in the quest for environmental security.

Today Earth is under threat from a variety of directions. Resources are rapidly disappearing or polluted, including fresh water, energy sources, vital minerals, forests, agriculturally productive land, and wildlife and fish stocks. There is worry about the thinning of Earth's ozone layer, which protects the planet from the sun's dangerous ultraviolet rays and allows human life to exist. The global-warming threat has also been making news headlines in the past few years.

But what of the poorer countries that want to advance economically? One of the key ingredients leading to the abject poverty of the Global South is the lack of an industrialized economic base. To raise the standard of living of the more than 5 billion people who live in LDCs, governments in these countries will have to build an industrial capacity similar to that of the wealthier North. Yet if Earth's capacity to support human life and industrialization as it currently exists is already under stress, how will it be able to withstand the future economic growth of the vastly populated Global South? How can the standard of living playing field finally be leveled for all of Earth's citizens, without destroying Earth itself? This is the conundrum behind the issue of "sustainable development." This term applies to the need for economic growth to be balanced with protecting the environment.

IT'S OUR TURN TO GROW: SUSTAINABLE DEVELOPMENT AND THE NORTH-SOUTH DIVIDE

Sustainable development became the popular catch phrase following the historic 1992 "Earth Summit," or the UN Conference on Environment and Development (UNCED) that took place in Rio de Janeiro, Brazil. UNCED was the largest gathering ever in UN history, reflecting the importance that the global community was placing on environmental concerns. Prior to the Rio meeting, the goals of global economic development and environmental protection were not linked together and, in fact, were considered to be mutually exclusive. To become more developed and industrialized meant that the environment would be sacrificed. Yet since 1992, the UN and its partners have sought to intertwine the two together into a single global imperative. The aim of sustainable development is incorporated as a major part of the UN's 2000 Millennium Development Goals and was reaffirmed at the 2002 World Summit held in Johannesburg, South Africa.

As shifting climate patterns and pollution threaten water, resources, crops, and the overall environment, the UN has stepped up to take action against the deterioration of the planet by organizing environmental summits, as well as implementing goals and programs to promote greener living. Here, a woman wearing a face mask cycles through polluted air in Lanzhou, China. China is on track to become the world's number one emitter of greenhouse gases, surpassing the United States as early as 2009.

As laudable as the aim of sustainable development is, the 1992 Rio conference immediately revealed the significant gulf that exists between the economically developed countries (EDCs) and the poorer LDCs. On the one hand, the North, having already attained a certain level of economic prosperity had now become more environmentally sensitive. However it is the EDCs, with only one-fifth of the world's population, that currently produce the lion's share of global pollution and consume much of the world's natural resources. The countries of the South ask: Why should the responsibility of saving the environment rest on our shoulders? Why don't we have the right to develop and to use our domestic resources in the same way that you did for centuries before us? Explained a Chinese energy specialist: "You try to tell the people of Beijing that they can't buy a car or an air-conditioner because of the global climate-change issue. It is just as hot in Beijing as it is in Washington, DC."[34]

The North maintains that while that may be the case, global survival hinges on whether the Global South can rein in spiraling development that ignores environmental safeguards. If hugely populous countries like China and India continue at present speeds of development and environmental destruction, they will be economically developed but Earth's ecosystem will have crashed. Fine, say the LDCs. We are too poor to accomplish sustainable development on our own. If the global environment is to be saved, then the EDCs must give us financial and technological assistance to achieve sustainability.

Ten years later, at the 2002 Johannesburg Summit (often dubbed "Earth Summit II"), many of these tensions remained. The intervening decade did not spur the changes that the Rio participants had hoped for. The EDCs, particularly the United States, maintain that it is up to the LDCs to self-impose environmentally sound practices related to their economic growth. There will be some financial assistance, but not nearly the amount called for by the EDCs.

THE TRUE TEST OF GLOBAL COOPERATION: RESPONDING TO CLIMATE CHANGE

The North-South wedge surrounding sustainable development cuts across nearly every environmental concern, and it is particularly observable in the UN debates regarding global warming. Although the scientific community debated for years as to whether there was a genuine pattern emerging, the majority of scientists and politicians now believe that the world's temperatures are gradually rising. The burning of fossil fuels, such as oil, coal, and natural gas, which advanced economies' need for cars, heating, and industrial production, produce "greenhouse gases." These gases, principally carbon dioxide, or CO_2, become concentrated in the atmosphere and act like a greenhouse roof, trapping Earth's heat in, rather than naturally allowing the heat to emanate into outer space and allow the planet to cool at night. Greenhouse-gas output has increased 70 percent since 1970 and could grow by 25 to 90 percent in the next 25 years.

The years 1998 and 2001 were the warmest years ever. If no action is taken, climate-change specialists believe that Earth's temperature could rise between two and nine degrees Fahrenheit. Already global warming has caused mass suffering from the skyrocketing number of natural disasters, including catastrophic flooding, earthquakes, hurricanes, droughts, wildfires, and deadly snowstorms. Millions of the world's citizens have been impacted, and tens of thousands have died. One billion could be made homeless in the next 50 years. Melting Arctic ice spurs rising sea levels, imperiling the very existence of island countries in the Pacific and low-lying territories elsewhere. Agricultural, hunting, and fishing zones are all shifting with the temperature changes and snow lines on mountains are changing.

In 1988, the UN Environment Program and the World Meteorological Organization (WMO), a UN specialized agency, formed the Intergovernmental Panel on Climate Change (IPCC). IPCC brings together a network of more than 2,000 scientists and climate-change experts from more than a hundred countries to focus on the issue of global warming. At the 1992 Rio conference, the IPCC's studies formed the basis of the Framework Convention on Climate Change that contained a nonbinding goal of limiting greenhouse-gas emissions to 1990 levels by 2000, a target which was not achieved.

International agreements, like the Kyoto Protocol, have widespread support from many countries who have signed it—except the United States. Claiming that the agreement didn't hold developing countries responsible for their carbon emissions, the U.S. government says it would damage its economy, and refused to sign it.

The 1997 Kyoto Protocol established specific obligatory targets for greenhouse-gas output. It relies on a complex formula attempting to set specific targets for the largest producers, including the United States and the European Union countries. Kyoto did not stipulate that LDCs would have to cut back on emissions in the early stages, but they should commit to later action. The protocol came into effect in 2005 (and will expire in 2012), with all of the European Union members, Australia,

(continues on page 114)

CAN PLANTING TREES SAVE THE WORLD?

Wangari Maathai grew up the daughter of Kenyan farmers in the 1940s. She vividly recalls a landscape in Mount Kenya's highlands that was lush with trees, had plentiful crops for eating, and ample clean water. Upon returning to her homeland in the early 1970s following undergraduate and postgraduate studies in the United States and Europe, Maathai discovered a countryside very different from what she had remembered. Tea and coffee plantations, major cash crops for export, had taken over the productive agricultural fields and abundant forests of her youth, rivers were polluted with heavy silt, and her fellow Kenyans and their livestock that lived in the rural areas were malnourished. Landslides were common.

Maathai realized that it was the absence of the trees of her childhood, causing devastating soil erosion, that was at the heart of this crisis. As Maathai explains: "Now it was one thing to understand the issues. It is quite another to do something about them. But I have always been interested in finding solutions. This is, I believe, a result of my education as well as my time in America: to think of what can be done rather than worrying about what cannot. I didn't sit down and ask myself, 'Now let me see; what shall I do?' It just came to me: 'Why not plant trees?'"*

Maathai would go on to win the 2004 Nobel Peace Prize in recognition of her work with the "Green Belt Movement" that planted nearly 30 million trees on the African continent. Now Maathai has set her sights on an even bigger challenge: combating global warming. In November 2006, she announced the "Billion Tree" campaign during the UN Convention on Climate Change conference held in Kenya. In the Billion Tree Campaign, the UN Environment Program (UNEP) hosts a Web site at which anyone—from first-grade students to multinational corporations and national governments—can make a pledge to plant a tree. The goal was to have one billion pledged, verified by UNEP, by the end of 2007.

Trees are at the forefront of combating global warming. More than 80 percent of the world's natural forests have disappeared in a process known as deforestation. Earth's largest rain-forest regions in Brazil and Indonesia are being destroyed by damaging logging and agricultural practices. The environmental impact of chopping or burning down trees is twofold. First, the act of cutting them releases two major greenhouse gases, carbon dioxide and methane. Second, live trees naturally absorb carbon dioxide, which helps alleviate the greenhouse effect.

At a news conference following the Billion Tree campaign, Maathai, whose Green Belt Movement is one of the patrons of the UNEP effort, explained: "People talk too much. We are no longer talking, we are working. . . . The challenge now is to tell the world to go dig holes and plant seedlings. I've no doubt we will achieve our goal."[**] It turns out Maathai was right. UNEP achieved its goal of one billion trees seven months ahead of schedule, following a pledge of 20 million trees by the African country of Senegal.

The Billion Tree Campaign Web site can be found at http://www.unep.org/billiontreecampaign.

---

[*] Wangari Maathai, *Unbowed: A Memoir*. New York: Anchor Books, 2006, p. 125.

[**] "UN Wins Pledge to Plant a Billion Trees," MSNBC.com, 22 May 2007. Also available online at *http://www.msnbc.com/id/959700/displaymode/1176/rotary/18803155*.

(continued from page 111)

Canada, Japan, and Russia as parties. The United States, under the Bush administration, has steadfastly refused to join, protesting that Kyoto did not require major polluting LDCs, such as China and India, to make the same pledge. Implementing the targets, Washington asserts, would hurt the U.S. economy. Currently the North's 15 percent of the world's population produces more than 52 percent of CO_2 emissions. However if the South achieves the same level of industrialization as the North, global CO_2 output would increase 342 percent.

Secretary-General Ban Ki-moon has made the climate-change issue one of his top priorities. In advance of the 62nd General Assembly opening in September 2007, the secretary-general hosted 150 countries for a special one-day meeting on the topic. Climate change was also the central theme of the following General Assembly session, with more than 80 countries represented by their leaders, including President Bush. Secretary-General Ban has also appointed three special envoys on climate change to continue to press the issue with the world's governments.

In October 2007, the Nobel Peace Prize was awarded to former U.S. Vice President Al Gore and the UN's Intergovernmental Panel on Climate Change for their work in drawing the world's attention to the global-warming crisis. The Nobel Committee cited the IPCC's pivotal work in mobilizing awareness:

> Through the scientific reports it has issued over the past two decades, the IPCC has created an ever-broader informed consensus about the connection between human activities and global warming. Thousands of scientists and officials from over one hundred countries have collaborated to achieve greater certainty as to the scale of the warming. Whereas in the 1980s global warming seemed to be merely an interesting hypothesis, the 1990s produced firmer evidence in its support.

In the last few years, the connections have become even clearer and the consequences still more apparent.[35]

In December 2007, more than 180 countries gathered in Bali, Indonesia, to update the Kyoto Protocol standards. Within the United States, many state governors and city mayors had already decided to voluntarily follow Kyoto's guidelines, including Governor Arnold Schwarzenegger of California and New York City's Michael Bloomberg. Mayor Bloomberg even attended the Bali gathering. As he explained: "It's time for America to re-establish its leadership on all issues of international importance, including climate change. . . . Because if we are going to remain the world's moral compass, a role that we played throughout the 20th century—not always perfectly but pretty darn well—we need to regain our footing on the world stage."[36]

Public awareness and pressure for change has dramatically increased across the world. As Achim Steiner, Executive Director of UNEP, believes: "We have but a short time to avert damaging and economically debilitating climate change. The solutions are numerous and, as many economists say, affordable when compared with the cost of complacency."[37]

The UN:
Its Predicaments
and Promise

With all the defects, with all the failures that we can check up against it, the UN still represents man's best-organized hope to substitute the conference table for the battlefield.[38]

—U.S. President Dwight Eisenhower,
former military general

IT IS OFTEN SAID THAT IF THERE WERE NO UN, SOMEONE would have to invent it. It would be difficult for even the UN's harshest critics to envision a world, particularly the immensely interdependent one of the twenty-first century, where no such body existed. When a highly infectious disease breaks out, who will respond to the alarm? What body will help when warring parties have decided to lay their guns down and want to talk, perhaps for the first time in decades? And once the peace is settled, what institution will arrive to help rebuild society? Where should the world's countries meet to forge new policies to address the myriad transnational problems like poverty, climate change, overpopulation, HIV/AIDS, terrorism, human trafficking, human rights, and war? More importantly, who will implement these policies worldwide day to day and for years to come?

Still even the UN's strongest supporters will acknowledge that the United Nations, as designed, is not the perfect answer to world peace. Individuals who work within the organization and its passionate advocates among the outside public are the first to recognize that there are genuine issues hampering the UN from fulfilling its ultimate promise. The UN is under-funded and understaffed, nowhere near sufficiently equipped in resources to address the many profound challenges in today's international society. Its more than 60-year-old deci-sion-making mechanisms, particularly the Security Council, are also in desperate need of reform. In its starkest relief, people cry out for help in Myanmar and Darfur, Sudan, adding to the unheard pleas of Bosnians and Rwandans before them, and the Security Council's five permanent powers negotiate their fates amongst themselves.

Still there is no UN without its member countries. If the UN is to reach its fullest potential, the responsibility for change lies largely with the governments of the world, not the organi-zation. And it is the world's citizens, the greatest beneficiaries of the UN's efforts, who must be vigilant in keeping their respec-tive governments focused on this pursuit. "The world needs skeptical intelligence and vision,"[39] writes veteran international observer Paul Kennedy.

Within the United States, many Americans have strong opinions about the UN, in both the "for" and "against" categories. In an informal June 2007 poll taken by *Parade* magazine, 25,000 readers were asked: "Does the UN still matter?" A startling 71 percent responded no while only 29 percent said yes.[40] Those who believed in the importance of the UN highlighted its role in everything from natural disasters and disease responses, to helping refugees and keeping communication channels open between countries, which has prevented World War III. Its detractors stated that the world's countries simply ignore the UN's mandates and pursue their own national agendas, while the organization itself is corrupt and wasteful.

Yet those that have represented the United States in world affairs, on both sides of the political divide, frequently champion the importance of the world body for the achievement of American interests. Former President Bill Clinton's secretary of state and UN ambassador, Madeline Albright, asserts that:

> You may think that you have never benefited personally from the UN . . . but if you have ever traveled on an international airline or shipping line, or placed a phone call overseas, or received mail from outside the country, or been thankful for an accurate weather report—then you have been served directly or indirectly by one part or another of the UN system.[41]

John Negroponte, a former U.S. ambassador to the United Nations under the Bush administration and later his deputy secretary of state, explains it this way:

> I'm struck by how relevant the work that I've had to do at the UN has been to the U.S. national security and foreign policy agenda. Part of our debate here in the U.S. has always turned around the issue of what does the UN mean to me? My answer to any American today

is it means as much as national security and foreign policy should mean to you.[42]

If the UN is to succeed, America's support is indispensable. Recall that it was two American presidents, at different times in world history, who led the call for a global institution addressing the great problems of war and peace. Presidents Wilson and Roosevelt both recognized that while the United States may be an important power, it can only achieve a safe, healthy, and free world in concert with others. As Stephen Schlesinger concludes in his seminal history on the UN, *Act of Creation*, the United States "must now find its way back to one of its greatest creations. The process must begin anew—for the fate of our country, our world and our future."[43]

Young Americans are therefore in the driver's seat when it comes to the United Nations. They must empower themselves with knowledge about the faults and prospects of the organization and move it forward accordingly. The future of the UN, and by extension, the quest to achieve a world finally free from fear, is in their hands.

1918   World War I ends.

1920   The League of Nations starts.

1945   United Nations Conference on International
        Organization is held in San Francisco from April
        through June.

        World War II ends.

        The United Nations legally enters into existence on
        October 24; celebrated annually as United Nations
        Day.

1946   UN General Assembly holds its first meeting with 51
        member countries participating.

1948   UN General Assembly adopts Universal Declaration
        of Human Rights.

1950   With Soviet Union absent, the UN Security Council
        authorizes first collective military response against
        North Korea upon its invasion of South Korea.

        UN wins first of nine Nobel Peace Prizes, recognizing
        the work of Ralph Bunche, the UN acting mediator
        for the Israeli-Arab conflict.

1956   UN Emergency Force, the first official UN
        peacekeeping mission, is authorized for Suez Canal
        crisis.

1961   While on a UN diplomatic mission to the Congo,
        Secretary-General Dag Hammarskjöld is killed in a
        plane crash.

1971   UN General Assembly recognizes the People's
        Republic of China for the first time. The Republic of
        China (Taiwan) is no longer represented at the UN.

1990   For only the second time in its history, and this time with all five permanent members of the Security Council approving, the UN authorizes collective military measures against Iraq after its invasion of Kuwait.

1991   The Soviet Union legally disappears from existence. Russia assumes the former USSR's seat on the UN Security Council and in the other main bodies.

1994   Palau, the last UN Trust Territory, becomes independent and joins the UN as its newest member.

2000   Following the UN Millennium Summit, landmark Millennium Development Goals (MDG) are adopted.

2003   The International Criminal Court, the world's first permanent war crimes tribunal, begins operations.

2006   Montenegro becomes the one hundred ninety-second member of the UN.

        Secretary-General Kofi Annan steps down following the end of his second term. Ban Ki-moon of South Korea is appointed the next secretary-general.

2007   The UN's Intergovernmental Panel on Climate Change and former U.S. vice president Al Gore win the Nobel Peace Prize for their efforts to draw the world's attention to the impact of global warming. Secretary-General Ban Ki-moon makes climate change his top policy priority.

Chapter 1

1. "Acceptance Speech by H.E. Mr. Ban Ki-moon on Appointment as the 8th Secretary-General of the United Nations," October 13, 2006. Available online at *http://www.unsgselection.org/files/BankiMoon_Acceptance Speech_13Oct06.pdf*.

Chapter 2

2. Erich Maria Remarque, *All Quiet on the Western Front*. New York: Fawcett Crest, 1975, p. 263.

Chapter 3

3. Stephen Schlesinger, "Text of President Truman's Address, Bringing the World Peace Parley to An End" in *Act of Creation: The Founding of The United Nations*. Cambridge, Mass.: Westview Press, 2004, p. 290.

4. "An Oral History Account of the Founding of the United Nations." Available online at *http://www.yale.edu/unsy/Oralhist/krasno/oral_history.html*.

5. "On This Day: January 11, 1946," *Times of London*, January 11, 2000.

Chapter 4

6. Linda Fasulo, *An Insider's Guide to the UN*. New Haven, Conn.: Yale University Press, 2004, p. 9.

7. Ibid., p. 92.

8. Timothy Wirth, "A Multi-Lateral Moment: The Golden Opportunity of the U.S.-UN Relationship," Address to the George Washington University Elliot School of International Affairs, March 7, 2007. Available online at *http://unfoundation.org/files/pdf/2007/US_UN _Relationship_Elliot_School_speech3707.pdf*.

9. Fasulo, pp. 92–93.

10. Wilfred Grey, *U.N. Jigsaw.* New York: Vantage Press, 2000, p. 36.

11. Fasulo, p. 96.

12. Ibid.

13. Ibid., p. 148.

14. Boutros Boutros-Ghali, "Global Leadership After the Cold War," *Foreign Affairs*, 75, no. 2 (1996), p. 98.

15. Ian Johnstone, "The Role of the UN Secretary-General: The Power of Persuasion Based on Law," *Global Governance*, no. 9 (2003), p. 444.

16. *The International Court of Justice: Questions and Answers about the Principal Organ of the United Nations.* New York: UN Department of Public Information, 2000, p. 22.

17. Ibid., p. 12

18. Ibid., p. 25

19. Grey, p. 40.

20. Quoted in Thomas G. Weiss, Tatiana Carayannis, Louis Emmerij and Richard Jolly, *UN Voices: The Struggle for Development and Social Justice.* Bloomington, Ind.: Indiana University Press, 2005, p. 359.

Chapter 5

21. Boutros Boutros-Ghali, *An Agenda for Peace.* New York: United Nations, 1992, p. 45.

22. Quoted in *The United Nations in Our Daily Lives.* New York: United Nations, 1998, p. 5.

23. "Ex-peacekeepers Face Families and Victims of Bosnia Massacre," *International Herald Tribune*, October 17, 2007. Also available online at *http://www.iht.com/articles/2007/10/17/asia/serbs.php*.

24. "Comprehensive Three-Year Study Shows Surprising Evidence of Major Declines in Armed Conflicts, Genocides, Human Rights Abuse, Military Coups and International

Crises Worldwide," Human Security Centre, Liu Institute for Global Issues, University of British Columbia. Available online at *http://www.humansecurityreport.info/content/view/31/36/*.

Chapter 6

25. Available online at *http://www.un.org/News/dh/latest/nobelpage.htm*.
26. Charles W. Kegley, Jr., *World Politics: Trend and Transformation*. Boston, Mass.: Thomson Wadsworth, 2008, p. 130.
27. Lawrence Ziring, Robert Riggs, and Jack Plano, *The United Nations*. Boston, Mass.: Thomson-Wadsworth, 2005, pp. 471–477.
28. Kegley, Jr., p.143.
29. *The United Nations in Our Daily Lives*. p. 17.
30. Freedom House, *The Worst of the Worst: The World's Most Repressive Societies 2007*. New York: Freedom House, 2007. Available online at *http://www.freedomhouse.org/uploads/special_report/58.pdf*, p. 1.
31. John T. Rourke, *International Politics on the World Stage*. New York: McGraw-Hill, 2007, p. 288.
32. "ICTY at a Glance," International Criminal Tribunal for Former Yugoslavia, United Nations. Available online at *http://www.un.org/icty/glance-e/index.htm*.

Chapter 7

33. *The United Nations in Our Daily Lives*. p. 20.
34. "China's Inevitable Dilemma: Coal Equals Growth," *The New York Times*, November 29, 1995, p. A1.
35. Press Release, "The Nobel Peace Prize for 2007." Available online at *http://nobelprize.org/nobel_prizes/peace/laureates/2007/press.html*.

36. "Mayor Bloomberg to Attend U.N. Meeting on Climate Change," *The New York Times*, November 3, 2007. Also available online at *http://www.newyorktimes.com*.

37. United Nations Environment Program, The Billion Tree Campaign. Available on line at *http://www.unep.org/billiontreecampaign*.

Chapter 8

38. Schlesinger, p. 287.

39. Paul Kennedy, *The Parliament of Man: The Past, Present, and Future of the United Nations*. New York: Random House, 2006, p. 39.

40. *Parade*, October 14, 2007, p. 15.

41. Fasulo, p. 13.

42. Ibid., p. 13.

43. Schlesinger, p. 287.

BIBLIOGRAPHY

"Acceptance Speech by H.E. Mr. Ban Ki-moon on Appointment as the 8th Secretary-General of the United Nations," United Nations. Available online. URL: http://www.unsgselection. org/files/BankiMoon_AcceptanceSpeech_13Oct06.pdf.

Ban, Ki-moon. "Why the World Has Changed in the UN's Favor." *Newsweek International*, (June 4, 2007). Available online. URL: http://www.un.org/sg/press_article.html.

Beah, Ishmael. A *Long Way Gone: Memoirs of a Boy Soldier*. New York: Sarah Crichton Books, 2007.

"The Billion Tree Campaign," United Nations Environment Program. Available online. URL: http://www.unep.org/billiontreecampaign.

Boutros-Ghali, Boutros. *An Agenda for Peace*. New York: United Nations, 1992.

———. "Global Leadership After the Cold War," *Foreign Affairs* 75, 2 (March/April 1996): pp. 86–98.

"Child Soldiers," Amnesty International Homepage. Available online. URL: http://www.web.amnesty.org/pages/childsoldiers-index-eng.

"China's Inevitable Dilemma: Coal Equals Growth." *The New York Times*, November 29, 1995, p. A1.

"Comprehensive Three-Year Study Shows Surprising Evidence of Major Declines in Armed Conflicts, Genocides, Human Rights Abuse, Military Coups and International Crises Worldwide," Human Security Centre, Liu Institute for Global Issues, University of British Columbia. Available online. URL: http://www.humansecurityreport.info/content/view/31/36/.

"Does the UN Still Matter?" *Parade*. October 14, 2007, p. 15.

"Ex-peacekeepers Face Families and Victims of Bosnia Massacre." *International Herald Tribune*, October 17,

2007. Available online. URL: http://www.iht.com/arti-cles/2007/10/17/asia/serbs.php.

Fasulo, Linda. *An Insider's Guide to the UN*. New Haven, Conn.: Yale University Press, 2004.

Freedom House. *The Worst of the Worst: The World's Most Repressive Societies 2007*. New York: Freedom House, 2007. Available online. URL: http://www.freedomhouse.org/uploads/special_report/58.pdf.

Grey, Wilfred. *U.N. Jigsaw*. New York: Vantage Press, 2000.

"ICTY at a Glance," United Nations. Available online. URL: http://www.un.org/icty/glance-e/index.htm.

The International Court of Justice. New York: UN Department of Public Information, 2000.

Johnstone, Ian. "The Role of the UN Secretary-General: The Power of Persuasion Based on Law." *Global Governance* 9 (2003): pp. 441–458.

Kegley, Charles, Jr. *World Politics: Trend and Transformation*. Boston, Mass.: Thomson-Wadsworth, 2008.

Kennedy, Paul. *The Parliament of Man: The Past, Present, and Future of the United Nations*. New York: Random House, 2006.

Maathai, Wangari. *Unbowed: A Memoir*. New York: Anchor Books, 2006.

"Mayor Bloomberg to Attend U.N. Meeting on Climate Change." *The New York Times*, November 3, 2007. Available online. URL: http://www.newyorktimes.com.

McConnell, Tristan. "All-Female Unit Keeps Peace in Libe-ria," *PeaceWomen.Org*. Available online. URL: http://www.peacewomen.org/un/pkwatch/News/07/LiberianfemPK-ERS.html.

"Presentation Speech by Gunnar Berge, Chairman of the Nor-
    wegian Nobel Committee," NobelPrize.org. Available online.
    URL: http://www.nobelprize.org/nobel_prizes/peace/laure-
    ates/2001/presentation-speech.html.

"Press Release: The Nobel Peace Prize for 2007," NobelPrize.
    org. Available online. URL: http://nobelprize.org/nobel_
    prizes/peace/laureates/2007/press.html.

Remarque, Erich Maria. *All Quiet on the Western Front*. New
    York: Fawcett Crest, 1975.

Rourke, John T. *International Politics on the World Stage*. New
    York: McGraw-Hill, 2007.

Schlesinger, Stephen. *Act of Creation: The Founding of the
    United Nations*. Cambridge, Mass.: Westview Press, 2004.

"UN Wins Pledge to Plant a Billion Trees," MSNBC.com. May
    22, 2007. Available online. URL: http://www.msnbc.com/
    id/959700/displaymode/1176/rotary/18803155.

The United Nations in Our Daily Lives. New York: United
    Nations, 1998.

"War-torn childhood 'A Long Way Gone,' but not forgotten,"
    USATODAY.com. February 14, 2007. Available online. URL:
    http://www.usatoday.com/life/books/news/2007-02-14-
    beah-book_x.htm.

"We Can Love What We Are, Without Hating What—And
    Who—We Are Not: Secretary-General Says in Nobel Lec-
    ture," United Nations. Available online. URL: http://www.
    un.org/News/dh/latest/nobelpage.htm.

Weiss, Thomas G., Tatiana Carayannis, Louis Emmerij, and
    Richard Jolly. *UN Voices: The Struggle for Development
    and Social Justice*. Bloomington, Ind.: Indiana University
    Press, 2005.

Wirth, Timothy. "A Multi-Lateral Moment: The Golden
    Opportunity of the U.S.-UN Relationship," Address to the

George Washington University, Elliot School of International Affairs, March 7, 2007, United Nations Foundation. Available online. URL: http://unfoundation.org/files/pdf/2007/US_UN_Relationship_Elliot_School_speech3707.pdf.

Women, Peace and Security: Study Submitted by the Secretary-General Pursuant to Security Council Resolution 1325 (2000). New York: United Nations, 2002. Available online. URL: http://www.unicef.org/emerg/files/wps.pdf.

"World Assembly Begins Its Task: On This Day; 11 January 1946." *The Times* (London), January 11, 2000. Available online. URL: http://www.lexisnexis.com.

Yale University. United Nations Oral History Project. *An Oral History Account of the Founding of the United Nations.* Available online. URL: http://www.yale.edu/unsy/Oralhist/krasno/oral_history.html.

Ziring, Lawrence, Robert Riggs, and Jack Plano. *The United Nations.* Boston, Mass.: Thomson-Wadsworth, 2005.

FURTHER READING

Basic Facts About the United Nations. New York: The United Nations, 2004.

Beah, Ishmael. *A Long Way Gone: Memoirs of a Boy Soldier*. New York: Sarah Crichton Books, 2007.

Claude, Inis. *Swords Into Plowshares: The Problems and Progress of International Organization*. New York: Random House, 1984.

Dallaire, Romeo. *Shake Hands With the Devil: The Failure of Humanity in Rwanda*. New York: Avalon Publishing Group, 2004.

Fasulo, Linda. *An Insider's Guide to the UN*. New Haven, Conn.: Yale University Press, 2004.

Hoopes, Townsend and Douglas Brinkley. *FDR and the Creation of the UN*. New Haven, Conn.: Yale University Press, 1997.

Grey, Wilfred. *U.N. Jigsaw*. New York: Vantage Press, 2000.

Kennedy, Paul. *The Parliament of Man: The Past, Present, and Future of the United Nations*. New York: Random House, 2006.

Knock, Thomas J. *To End All Wars: Woodrow Wilson and the Quest for a New World Order*. Princeton, N.J.: Princeton University Press, 1992.

Maathai, Wangari. *Unbowed: A Memoir*. New York: Anchor Books, 2006.

Meisler, Stanley. *United Nations: The First Fifty Years*. New York: Grove Atlantic Press, 1995.

Mingst, Karen A. and Margaret Karns. *The United Nations in the 21st Century*. Boulder, Colo.: Westview Press, 2007.

Schlesinger, Stephen. *Act of Creation: The Founding of the United Nations*. Cambridge, Mass.: Westview Press, 2004.

The United Nations in Our Daily Lives. New York: United Nations, 1998.

Weiss, Thomas G., Tatiana Carayannis, Louis Emmerij, and Richard Jolly. *UN Voices: The Struggle for Development and Social Justice*. Bloomington, Ind.: Indiana University Press, 2005.

Williams, Ian. *The U.N. for Beginners*. New York: Writers and Readers Publishers, 1995.

Ziring, Lawrence, Robert Riggs, and Jack Plano. *The United Nations*. Boston, Mass: Thomson-Wadsworth, 2005.

WEB SITES

Amnesty International
http://www.amnesty.org.

The Better World Campaign
http://www.betterworldcampaign.org.

Citizens for Global Solutions
http://www.globalsolutions.org.

Freedom House
http://www.freedomhouse.org.

Human Rights Watch
http://www.hrw.org.

Security Council Report
http://www.securitycouncilreport.org.

UN CyberSchoolBus
http://cyberschoolbus.un.org.

UN Wire
http://www.unwire.org.

United Nations
http://www.un.org.

United Nations Association of the USA
http://www.unausa.org.

United Nations Children's Fund
http://www.unicef.org.

United Nations Foundation
http://www.unfoundation.org.

United States Mission to the United Nations
http://www.un.int/usa.

PICTURE CREDITS

INDEX

DR. KIRSTEN NAKJAVANI BOOKMILLER is a professor of government and political affairs at Millersville University of Pennsylvania, where she specializes in international law and organization, particularly humanitarian issues. She also serves as director of the university's Office of Global Education and Partnerships. Dr. Nakjavani Bookmiller received her B.A. in foreign service and international politics from Pennsylvania State University and her M.A. and Ph.D. in foreign affairs from the University of Virginia.

Series editor **PEGGY KAHN** is a professor of political science at the University of Michigan-Flint. She teaches world and European politics. She has been a social studies volunteer in the Ann Arbor, Michigan, public schools, and she helps prepare college students to become teachers. She has a Ph.D. in political science from the University of California, Berkeley, and a B.A. in history and government from Oberlin College.